TRAINING Grundwissen ENGLISCH

Mayer • Zieger

Englisch 10. Klasse
Aufgaben mit Lösungen

Bildnachweis

S. 3: © Khaane/www.khaane.com
S. 7: © ullstein/ullstein bild
S. 11: © Cinetext/Allstar
S. 13: © Gerd E. G. Paulsen/www.sxc.hu
S. 16: © Bradley Mason/www.sxc.hu
S. 26: © Paul Leach/www.sxc.hu
S. 46: © Sorin Brinzei
S. 49: © Cinetext
S. 52: © Cinetext
S. 55: © ullstein/Camera Press Ltd.
S. 61: © Dirk de Kegel 2004 (Sabam Belgium), www.sxc.hu
S. 63: © Cinetext/Allstar
S. 78: © Cinetext/Allstar
S. 82: © Disney/Cinetext
S. 83: © Stefan Diel/www.dlrptour.de
S. 84: © ullstein/ullstein bild
S. 89: © Disney/Cinetext
S. 102: © Cinetext
S. 122: © Cinetext/Allstar
S. 124: © David Hewitt/www.sxc.hu
S. 125: © Ralph Kiesewetter
S. 128: © J. C. Outrequin
S. 129: © Gerold Marks, Berlin

ISBN 978-3-89449-364-6

© 2010 by Stark Verlagsgesellschaft mbH & Co. KG
www.stark-verlag.de
1. Auflage 1999

Das Werk und alle seine Bestandteile sind urheberrechtlich geschützt. Jede vollständige oder teilweise Vervielfältigung, Verbreitung und Veröffentlichung bedarf der ausdrücklichen Genehmigung des Verlages.

Inhalt

Vorwort

... rund ums Nomen ... 1
1   Präpositionen ... 1
2   Adjektive ... 15
2.1   Einsatzmöglichkeiten von Adjektiven ... 15
2.2   Adjektive – Steigerung und Vergleiche ... 17

... rund ums Verb ... 23
3   Adverbien ... 23
3.1   Formen der Adverbien ... 23
3.2   Adjektiv oder Adverb nach bestimmten Verben ... 28
3.3   Stellung der Adverbien im Satz ... 31
4   Zeitformen des Verbs ... 35
4.1   *present tense* ... 35
4.2   *past tense* ... 41
4.3   *present perfect* ... 44
4.4   *past perfect* ... 50
4.5   *future tense* ... 52
5   Passiv ... 57
5.1   Formen des Passivs ... 57
5.2   Verschiedene Arten von Passivsätzen ... 60
6   Modale Hilfsverben ... 68
6.1   *can / could* ... 68
6.2   *may / might* ... 71
6.3   *will / would* ... 72
6.4   *shall / should* ... 74
6.5   *must / mustn't / needn't* ... 75
7   Gerundium ... 80
8   Infinitiv ... 90
8.1   Verwendung des Infinitivs ... 90
8.2   Gerundium oder Infinitiv? ... 102

Fortsetzung siehe nächste Seite

	... rund um den Satz	**107**
9	Indirekte Rede	107
10	Relativsätze	119
11	Sprechabsichten	123
12	Textproduktion	130
12.1	Briefe	130
12.2	E-Mails	133
12.3	*Summary*	134

Lösungen **137**

Autoren: Alois Mayer, Gillian Zieger
Illustrator: Igor Schulz-Bertram

Vorwort

Liebe Schülerin, lieber Schüler,

wenn du manchmal das Gefühl hast, im Englischunterricht nicht richtig mitzukommen, und wenn du deine Noten in diesem Fach verbessern willst, so wird dir das vorliegende Buch eine ideale Hilfe sein, den Englischstoff der 10. Klasse zu bewältigen. Anhand von ausführlichen und klar verständlichen Erklärungen, einleuchtenden Beispielen und zahlreichen Übungen kannst du mit diesem Buch die wichtigsten Gebiete der englischen Grammatik selbstständig erarbeiten.

- Jedes Kapitel beginnt mit **schülergerechten Erklärungen und Regeln** zum jeweiligen Grammatikbereich. Die theoretischen Ausführungen werden durch Beispiele verdeutlicht, sodass der Anwendungsbezug immer sichtbar bleibt.

- An die Theorie schließen sich **vielfältige Übungen** an, bei deren Bearbeitung du siehst, ob du das grammatische Phänomen begriffen hast und in die Praxis umsetzen kannst. Die Aufgaben sind oft illustriert und befassen sich inhaltlich mit einer großen Bandbreite von Themen. Die mit einem * gekennzeichneten Aufgaben sind die besonders schwierigen. Diese können für dich eine echte Herausforderung darstellen.

- Anhand des ausführlichen **Lösungsteils** kannst du deine Ergebnisse selbstständig überprüfen und deine Fortschritte kontrollieren.

Du kannst dieses Buch als ergänzende Vorbereitungshilfe für **Klassenarbeiten bzw. Schulaufgaben** verwenden oder damit den gesamten Lehrstoff wiederholen, wenn du für eine **Nachprüfung** im Fach Englisch lernen musst.

Wir wünschen dir viel Erfolg und Freude bei der Arbeit mit diesem Buch!

Alois Mayer   Gillian Zieger

... rund ums Nomen

1 Präpositionen

Präpositionen *(prepositions)* sind Wörter wie *on, until, across*. Du verwendest Präpositionen, wenn du

- ein **Verhältnis des Ortes** oder der **Richtung**
  Beispiel: Alan is standing <u>at</u> the entrance of the swimming pool.
- ein **Verhältnis der Zeit**
  Beispiel: I have been living here <u>since</u> 1997.
- oder ein **anderes Verhältnis**
  Beispiel: Peter went to the party <u>with</u> his girlfriend.

beschreiben möchtest.

Für die Verwendung von Präpositionen gibt es im Englischen nur wenige Regeln. Du solltest daher jedes Auftauchen einer Präposition als Einzelfall ansehen, im Wörterbuch nachschlagen und auswendig lernen.

Rund um Präpositionen des Ortes und der Richtung

Präpositionen des Ortes *(prepositions of place)*

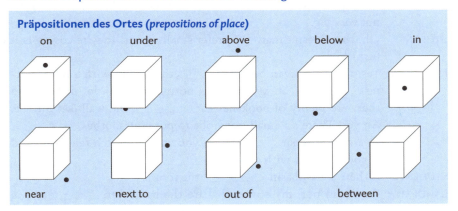

on — under — above — below — in

near — next to — out of — between

2 ... rund ums Nomen: Präpositionen

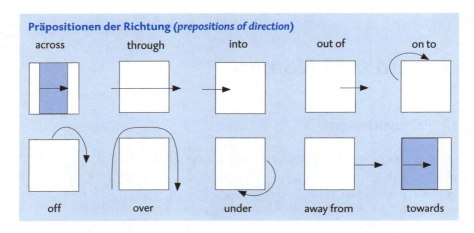

Aufgabe 1 Room to let: Put in the missing prepositions in the following telephone conversation.

LANDLADY: 573120
STUDENT: Hello. Is that Mrs Harrison?
LANDLADY: Yes, that's right.
STUDENT: Good morning. My name's Gillian Clarke. I was given your address by the Student Accommodation Agency. I was told you had a room to let.
LANDLADY: Yes, I've got one vacant room left. It's an attic room _____ the top of the house, _____ the second floor. I'm afraid it's not very big.
STUDENT: Oh, that doesn't matter! I prefer small rooms, they're cosier! Is it furnished?
LANDLADY: Yes, there's a divan bed _____ the corner with a new mattress _____ it. My students normally have a lot of books so there are plenty of bookshelves _____ the wall. Let me see. Ah yes! There's a small wardrobe to put your clothes _____, an armchair to sit _____ if you want to watch television and of course a desk with a lamp _____ it.
STUDENT: Is there a washbasin _____ the room?
LANDLADY: I'm afraid not, my students share the bathroom _____ the corridor. There's a washbasin, a shower and a bath. The toilet is separate. Unfortunately it's _____ the floor below.
STUDENT: I see. Is the room quiet?

LANDLADY: Oh, yes. It's _____ the back of the house, so you won't hear any noise from the traffic _____ the road.
STUDENT: Well, that sounds just what I'm looking for. May I come and see the room?
LANDLADY: Certainly! I'll be _____ home for the rest of the day.
STUDENT: Can you tell me how to get there?
LANDLADY: It's very easy. The tube station is _____ the Northern Line. Get off _____ Golders Green station. When you come out of the station, turn left and the house is _____ the third street _____ the right, 33 Seabrook Lane. You can't miss it. There's a church _____ the corner.
STUDENT: Thank you very much, Mrs Harrison. Goodbye.

Aufgabe 2   Guided Walks of London: Put in the missing prepositions.

While I was in London I took part in several interesting guided walks. One of them was discovering "The London of Jack the Ripper". Jack the Ripper was a murderer who terrorised Londoners in 1888. The walk started _____ Whitechapel Underground Station. When we set off _____ Whitechapel it was already beginning to get dark. The walk always takes place in the evening so that the participants can experience the atmosphere of London in Victorian times when the streets were gas-lit and strange shadows fell _____ the walls of the old houses. It was quite frightening walking through the dark, narrow streets where the murders took place. I found myself looking closely _____ every man who came _____ me. Suddenly someone fell _____ me. I screamed! Then I saw to my embarrassment that the "murderer" was only our guide who had tripped over a stone lying on the pavement. He smiled _____ me and said laughingly: "Did I give you a fright? I think the best thing to do now is to go _____ a drink. How about going _____ the 'Jack the Ripper' pub?" He pointed _____ a brightly-lit building at the end of the street. As we walked _____ the pub I had to laugh _____ myself!

Die folgenden Wendungen sind fest mit bestimmten Präpositionen verbunden. Du solltest sie und ihre deutsche Bedeutung auswendig lernen!

by land/sea/air	auf dem Land-, See-, Luftweg
by ship/plane/car/train etc.	mit dem Schiff, Flugzeug, Auto, Zug usw.
by heart	auswendig
by letter	schriftlich, brieflich
by post	auf dem Postweg
by accident/chance	zufällig, durch Zufall
by oneself/himself etc.	allein
by the way	übrigens
by sight	jdn. vom Sehen kennen
by name	dem Namen nach kennen
by far	bei weitem
in common	gemeinsam, gemeinschaftlich
in public	in der Öffentlichkeit
in secret	insgeheim
in debt	Schulden haben
in danger	in Gefahr
in other words	mit anderen Worten
in half/pieces	zur Hälfte, in Stücken
in the end	schließlich, zuletzt
in trouble	in Schwierigkeiten stecken, Ärger haben
in general	im Allgemeinen
in all	alles in allem
in the opinion of	nach Meinung
in turn	abwechselnd

on foot	zu Fuß
on purpose	absichtlich
on fire	brennen, in Brand
on a journey /trip	auf Reisen/auf einer Kurzreise
on the whole	im Ganzen gesehen
on strike	streiken
out of work	arbeitslos
out of this world	nicht in/von dieser Welt
out of turn	außer der Reihe
out of sight	außer Sicht sein, nicht mehr zu sehen
out of place	unangebracht, deplatziert

Aufgabe 3 Plastic Star: Translate the words in brackets into English.

He's world-famous and (nach Meinung) _____ of thousands of teenagers he's the best-looking boy they've ever seen. They know his songs (auswendig) _____. His photograph is on their bedroom walls. He's 22 years old. He's Duncan Deane and he's a star! A star, a pop-star, living in a shining, plastic world.

He wakes up in a luxury hotel room (allein) _____, and has his breakfast (im Bett) _____ at midday. Outside his hotel room, several hundred teenage girls are (weinen) _____. They hold up banners with the name Duncan written (in Farbe) _____ on them. They have something (gemeinsam) _____, they are all (verliebt) _____ with him. (Abwechselnd) _____ they try to push their way past the bored policemen. (Zufällig) _____ Duncan might be (in Sicht) _____. Every week there are different faces, different songs, but the same screams.

(Außer Sicht) _____ the Star finishes his breakfast, gets dressed and takes one last look in the mirror before he leaves his room. In the hotel lounge the reporters are waiting for him. With his pink suit and green hair Duncan looks (fehl am Platz) _____. He talks to the reporters but (tatsächlich) _____ he has nothing to say.

A car arrives at the back of the hotel. It's (bei weitem) _____ the biggest and most expensive one you can buy. The Star, his manager, his agent, his bodyguard and several girlfriends get in. The car takes them to a stadium where 8,000 teenage mouths are wide open and five hundred policemen's mouths are tightly shut. Ambulances wait (außer Sicht) _____. The Star waits in his dressing-room and finishes his fourth glass of whisky. He climbs the stairs to the stage and stands (in der Öffentlichkeit) _____ in the spotlight. (Für sich) _____ he wishes he were far away (im Urlaub) _____. He sings and there are 8,000 screams. He sings again. There are 16,000 tears in the teenage eyes. He stops singing. There's £1,000 in his manager's pocket.

He leaves the stage, goes (mit dem Auto) _____ to the airport and then (mit dem Flugzeug) _____ to the next hotel. (Übrigens) _____ there are several hundred teenagers waiting for him. He's a Star!

Adjektive, die häufig in Verbindung mit Präpositionen auftauchen:	
good at	gut in
hopeless at	hoffnungslos gegenüber
married to	verheiratet mit
similar to	ähnlich
keen on	sehr viel übrig haben für
different from	anders als, verschieden
rich in	reich an
dependent on	abhängig von
afraid of	Angst haben vor
proud of	stolz auf
sure/certain of	sich (einer Sache) sicher sein
full of	voll von
tired of	müde/überdrüssig, satt haben
tolerant/intolerant of	tolerant/intolerant gegenüber
capable/incapable of	fähig/unfähig zu
jealous of	eifersüchtig auf
ashamed of	sich schämen für, beschämt
Verben, die häufig in Verbindung mit Präpositionen auftauchen:	
look at	anschauen
stare at	anstarren
glance at	einen Blick werfen auf
laugh at	lachen über
aim at	zielen auf
point at	zeigen auf
speak to	sprechen mit
listen to	zuhören
write to	schreiben an
go to	gehen/fahren nach

travel to	reisen nach
apologise to (s.o.) for (sth.)	sich bei jemandem für etwas entschuldigen
explain (sth.) to (s.o.)	jemandem etwas erklären
prefer to	vorziehen zu
describe (sth.) to (s.o.)	jemandem etwas beschreiben
hand (sth.) to (s.o.)	jemandem etwas geben

Aufgabe 4 Henry VIII: Put in the missing prepositions.

Although I'm very interested _____ history, I'm not very good _____ remembering facts like the names of all the women Henry VIII was married _____. I know that he was keen _____ Anne Boleyn while still married _____ Catherine of Aragon. Henry was dependent _____ the Pope to give him permission to divorce Catherine. When the Pope refused, Henry started up his own Church which was typical _____ him. As you can guess, Henry's new Church, the Church of England, allowed divorces. He got rid of Catherine and married Anne but it wasn't long before Henry became tired _____ her so she was beheaded. Another of Henry's wives, Catherine Howard, suffered a fate similar _____ Anne's. She was also executed but I can't remember when, because I'm hopeless _____ remembering dates. As you know history is full _____ names and dates! Henry was very intolerant _____ women who were incapable _____ giving birth to sons! At last one of his six wives did in fact give him a son. Henry was very proud _____ his heir who succeeded his father at the age of nine. As he was too young to govern by himself the country was managed by his guardians who were constantly jealous _____ each other. The young king died at an early age and in the end it was a woman, Elizabeth I., who reigned over England and became one of the most famous queens in English history.

8 ... rund ums Nomen: Präpositionen

Aufgabe 5 Daniel's 16th Birthday Party: Put in the missing prepositions.

Daniel had decided to have a big party to celebrate his 16th birthday. He wanted it to be a really special occasion and started making plans weeks in advance. The main problem was how to explain _____ his parents that he would prefer to celebrate just with his friends. Perhaps he could persuade them to go away somewhere for the weekend. The trouble was, his parents were "stay _____ home" types who enjoyed a bit of gardening or sitting indoors listening _____ classical music. Daniel didn't want to offend them but he felt he was old enough to have a birthday party without his parents.

One evening at dinner, Daniel smiled _____ his mother and said: "Mum, when was the last time you and Dad went away together on your own?" Mrs Roberts glanced _____ her husband. "Ages ago", she answered, "it must have been well before you were born."

"Why do you want to know?" asked Mr Roberts staring in surprise _____ his son. Daniel took a deep breath and began to talk _____ his parents about his plans for his 16th birthday party. His parents listened _____ him without interrupting. When Daniel had finished, Mr Roberts stood up and said: "Your mother and I will have to think about this. We'll let you know our decision in a couple of days."

For the next few days Daniel was busy making arrangements. He had to make a shopping list and decide which of his friends he would invite _____ the party. Some of them he had to write _____ and others he could tell at school. He was so busy that he completely forgot about his parents.

Some days later he was upstairs in his room, listening _____ the CD he'd recently bought when he heard his father shouting _____ him from the bottom of the stairs. When Daniel came down he saw his father was holding a letter. "Here's our decision, Daniel", said Mr Roberts with a smile. He handed the letter _____ his son. Daniel opened it and read:

Dear Mrs Roberts,

We are pleased to inform you that you have won the first prize in our competition. A weekend for two in Paris for the 2nd and 3rd July! Congratulations!

When Daniel looked _____ the date he couldn't believe his eyes. It was exactly the weekend of his 16th birthday party.

... rund ums Nomen: Präpositionen 9

> Normalerweise stehen die Präpositionen vor ihrem Bezugswort. In bestimmten Fällen musst du die **Präposition** jedoch an das **Satzende** verschieben (nur in sehr formeller Sprache bleibt sie hier in ihrer Anfangsposition).
> - **Fragesätze**
>   Beispiel: What are you looking <u>at</u>?
> - **Relativsätze**
>   Beispiel: That's the boy Sarah's going out <u>with</u>.
> - **Passivsätze**
>   Beispiel: Do you know which country your watch was made <u>in</u>?

Aufgabe 6 Join the two sentences so that they make one sentence with the preposition at the end. It may be necessary to make some changes by leaving words out or adding words.

a) She gave the form to me. She asked me to fill it in.

b) Is this the purse? You were looking for it?

c) I like the people. I work with them.

d) Do you know this music? Who was it composed by?

e) Do you know the girl? Tom is talking to her.

f) That's the type of book. My father would be interested in it.

g) He's the boy. I told you about him.

h) She was operated on. When was it?

i) I've got lots of CDs. I never listen to them.

j) Yesterday I met a friend. I went to school with her.

_____

k) It's an invitation to a party. I've been invited to it.

_____

l) You are worried. What about?

_____

Rund um die Präpositionen der Zeit

Folgende *prepositions of time* solltest du auswendig kennen:

- *at* und *in*
  at verwendest du bei genauen Zeitangaben und bei Festtagen. Mit *in* drückst du eine längere Zeitdauer aus, z. B. Jahreszeiten, Jahre oder Tageszeiten.
  Beispiele: He came in <u>at</u> that moment.
  She was born <u>in</u> 1990.

- *since* und *for*
  since gibt einen Zeitpunkt an, *for* beschreibt hingegen eine Zeitdauer.
  Beispiele: I have been living here <u>since</u> 1995.
  I have been living here <u>for</u> three years.

- *on*
  on verwendest du zur Angabe von bestimmten Tagen und Daten.
  Beispiel: My birthday is <u>on</u> a Saturday this year.

- *by*
  Mit *by* drückt man einen bestimmten Zeitpunkt aus, zu dem eine Handlung abgeschlossen sein wird.
  Beispiel: He will probably arrive <u>by</u> 6 o'clock.

- *from … until*
  Mit *from* kannst du den Beginn einer Handlung angeben, mit *until (till, to)* das Ende der Handlung.
  Beispiel: I lived in London <u>from</u> 1990 <u>until</u> 1995.

Aufgabe 7 Elton John, Superstar: Put in the missing prepositions.

Elton John started life as Reg Dwight in a London suburb. _____ the age of four he learnt to play the piano and hasn't stopped playing _____ then. _____ his early days as a musician he earned one pound a night for playing the piano in a bar _____ weekends. Elton's career really started when he met the songwriter Bernie Taupin _____ 1967. They have been together _____ a long time and the combination of their talents has had all the right ingredients for success. The big break came _____ 1970 on Elton's first visit to the USA. One of Elton John's trademarks is his collection of glasses, glittery ones, colourful ones, enormous ones. He has a different pair for each occasion and probably wears an extra special pair _____ his birthday or _____ Christmas. Elton has been a superstar _____ the 70's _____ today. _____ the time he was 30 he was already a multi-millionaire. He rewrote his song 'Candle in the Wind' in commemoration of Princess Diana, who died after a car crash _____ the early hours of the morning _____ August 31st 1997. It has become the most successful single ever recorded.

Auch die folgenden Wendungen sind fest mit bestimmten Präpositionen verbunden. Du solltest sie und ihre deutsche Bedeutung auswendig lernen!

- Zusammensetzungen mit *at*
at the same time	gleichzeitig
at times	gelegentlich
at present	zur Zeit
at first	zuerst
at last	endlich

- Verbindungen mit *time*
in time	rechtzeitig
on time	pünktlich
behind the times	altmodisch
Once upon a time	Es war einmal …
in times of	in Zeiten von
for the time being	zurzeit

12 ... rund ums Nomen: Präpositionen

Aufgabe 8 Complete the following sentences with the correct expression.
a) I was learning the irregular verbs for an English exam, _____ my brother, who is 5 years younger, was watching television.
b) I'm reading a John Grisham novel _____. Do you want to borrow it when I've finished? It's really exciting.
c) _____ Charles and Diana seemed to be really happy but it wasn't long before things started going wrong between them.
d) _____ you're here. I've been waiting for ages!
e) _____ as I'm making the salad you can peel the potatoes.
f) My sister has taken her driving test 6 times but _____ she's passed it!
g) We've got a lot of exams to study for at the moment. _____ I wish I hadn't decided to stay on at school.
h) In Germany schools start much earlier than in Britain. _____ I found it very difficult to get up early in the morning but now I've got used to it.
i) Sorry I can't help you but I'm very busy _____.
j) When _____ the rescuers found him, he was nearly dead.
k) _____ he really gets on my nerves.
l) The unemployment rate in Germany is very high _____.

Aufgabe 9 Complete the sentences with the correct expression.
a) 'I'll meet you outside the cinema at 7.30.' OK, but please be _____.
b) I posted a birthday card to Jenny today. I hope it arrives _____.
c) In Britain, wearing school uniform prevents teenagers who can't afford the latest fashion in clothes from being laughed at and told that they are _____.
d) _____ there lived a beautiful princess. Her name was Goldenhair.
e) The International Red Cross and other charitable organisations send money, clothing and food to Third World countries _____ need.
f) I want to lose weight so I'm on a diet _____.

... rund ums Nomen: Präpositionen | 13

Aufgabe 10 The Life of a Cowboy: Put in the missing prepositions.

_____ the sun beats down on the dusty, deserted main street in No Name City, two figures face each other. _____ the street was full of life but now doors and shutters are firmly locked and eyes peer out from behind closed curtains, waiting _____ the danger is over. _____ some minutes a shot is heard and one of the men drops down dead. The other, the silver star on his chest glistening in the sunlight, slowly walks towards the saloon. Justice has won again.

Most of us are familiar with the Hollywood version of life in the 'Wild West' but what was the life of a cowboy really like? A lot of them were very different from the image portrayed by John Wayne or Gary Cooper. They were often young, unskilled labourers who, _____ they had come over to America, had to find the first job they could get. _____ they became cowboys many of them had been criminals.

The cowboy's life was hard. _____ most of the year he travelled thousands of miles driving the cows across lonely country to cattle markets. Horses were only a useful method of transport which had to be fed and watered but were ridden _____ they dropped.

_____ a trail drive the cowboy had to work 18 hours a day 7 days a week. The only time he could relax was _____ sitting around a campfire _____ he rolled up for the night in his bedroll _____ the first rays of sun woke him up the next morning.

The heyday of the cowboy was _____ the 1860's and 80's, _____ which time industrialisation gradually began to take over and the work of the cowboy was no longer needed.

14 ... rund ums Nomen: Präpositionen

Aufgabe 11 Components with "down". Tick off what is correct.

a) **Downtown** means
- [ ] business centre of a town or a city.
- [ ] a town at the foot of a hill.
- [ ] a town below sea level.

b) To **download** is
- [ ] to take out things of a car.
- [ ] to carry goods down into the cellar of a house.
- [ ] to move information or programs to a computer from TV or a telephone line.

c) A **downer** is
- [ ] somebody who cuts down trees and bushes.
- [ ] a drug that makes a person's mind and body less active.
- [ ] an excellent boxer.

d) He goes **down under** means
- [ ] he goes by underground.
- [ ] he goes to Australia or New Zealand.
- [ ] he can't swim.

Aufgabe 12 Homophone (A word which sounds the same as another but is different in meaning and spelling: **see** [siː] and **sea** [siː].

a) Fill in the correct words.
[raɪt] I must _____ a report. John writes plays for the stage. He is a play_____. Baptism is a religious _____. _____ or wrong?

[aːmz] The welcomed him with open _____. The soldiers laid down their _____. The poor people were given _____.

b) Which of the following pairs of words are not homophones? Underline the pairs.

disease	– decease	through	– threw
whole	– hole	seize	– cease
meat	– meet	flower	– flour
seam	– seem	tale	– tail

2 Adjektive

Adjektive *(adjectives)* sind Wörter wie *new, large, round*. Mit ihnen kannst du **Eigenschaften** oder **Merkmale** von **Lebewesen, Dingen, Begriffen, Zuständen** und **Tätigkeiten** näher beschreiben.

2.1 Einsatzmöglichkeiten von Adjektiven

An welche Stelle im Satz stellst du das Adjektiv?

- Das Adjektiv steht oft **vor dem Nomen**, zu dem es gehört (= attributiver Gebrauch). Es gibt einige Adjektive, die du ausschließlich so verwenden kannst. Dazu zählen *sick, habitual, former, occasional, hard, medical*.
  Beispiel: The <u>old car</u> over there is mine.

- Das Adjektiv kann aber auch **nach bestimmten Verben** – vor allem nach Formen von *to be* – stehen (= prädikativer Gebrauch). Einige Adjektive kannst du nur prädikativ verwenden. Hierzu gehören z. B. *well, ill, afraid, asleep*.
  Beispiel: My friend <u>is ill</u>.

- Mit vorangestelltem bestimmtem Artikel können Adjektive zur Bezeichnung einer **Gruppe** von Menschen verwendet werden. Nominal gebrauchte Adjektive werden wie Pluralformen behandelt, haben aber kein Plural-*s*: *The poor* (die Armen). Zur Bezeichnung einer oder mehrerer Einzelpersonen muss dem Adjektiv ein Nomen wie *man, woman, person, people* oder das Stützwort *one, ones* folgen (= attributiver Gebrauch, siehe oben).
  Beispiele: <u>The blind</u> must be helped.
  The boy helped the <u>blind man</u> across the street.

Aufgabe 1 Coca Cola – Many Big Businesses Start from Small Beginnings: Complete the sentences.

It was in Atlanta in 1886. Dr. John Pemberton owned a small laboratory where he produced all kinds of medicines. In his drugstore in 107, Marietta Street he sold his medicines to the _____ (Kranken) of Atlanta. He sold them mainly to the _____ (Armen) who could not afford to go to the doctor's. At that time, American doctors did not have a good reputation, so the _____ (Reichen) also bought their medicine in drugstores. The medicine Dr. Pemberton sold most was a brownish liquid for headaches containing the extracts of coca leaves – the beginnings of Coca Cola.

Europe, about 60 years later. During World War II, the American GIs brought Coca Cola, which had conquered the American continent, to Europe. The soft drink was often a kind of reward for the soldiers: the _____ (Tapferen) and the _____ (Mutigen) as well as the _____ (Verwundeten) received extra rations of Coke.

China, 1989. Four huge bottling plants had been built and the _____ / _____ (Neugierigen/Durstigen) lined up every morning to buy Coca Cola. Henceforth, the sweet lemonade could be bought all around the world.

Aufgabe 2 Early Coca Cola: Complete the sentences using the correct adjectives in brackets. (Use British English.)

When people were _____ (ill – sick) they often did not consult a doctor. They were _____ (afraid – frightened) by their high bills. The _____ (ill – sick) people went to the pharmacist's and bought their medicine there.

In Dr. Pemberton's forerunner of Coke, there was a small dose of cocaine which made the patients _____ (sleepy – asleep). After sleeping the patients felt _____ (good – well) for some time, but after some time their illness returned. _____ (healthy – well) people who were aware of this danger warned others. They were _____ (afraid – frightened) that habitual coke drinkers would become drug addicts.

At the turn of the century, the dose of cocaine was eliminated.

2.2 Adjektive – Steigerung und Vergleiche

Wie steigerst du Adjektive?

Die Steigerungsformen des Adjektivs, den **Komparativ** *(comparative)* und den **Superlativ** *(superlative)*, kannst du auf verschiedene Arten bilden:

- **Regelmäßige Steigerung**: Mit *-er/est* steigert man einsilbige Adjektive sowie zweisilbige Adjektive, die auf *-er, -le, -ow, -y* enden.

  Beispiele: high – high<u>er</u> – high<u>est</u>
  healthy – health<u>ier</u> – health<u>iest</u>

- **Steigerung mit *more/most***: Mit *more/most* steigert man zweisilbige Adjektive, die nicht auf *-er, -le, -ow, -y* enden, sowie drei- und mehrsilbige Adjektive.

  Beispiele: childish – <u>more</u> childish – <u>most</u> childish
  important – <u>more</u> important – <u>most</u> important

- **Unregelmäßige Steigerung**: Einige Adjektive werden mit Suppletivformen (Ersatzformen) gesteigert, d. h. die Steigerungsformen haben einen anderen Wortstamm als die Positivform.

  Beispiele:

Positiv	Komparativ	Superlativ
good	better	best
well	better	best
bad	worse	worst
ill	worse	worst
much	more	most
many	more	most
little	less	least

Bei der Übersetzung von ‚viel/viele' und ‚wenig/wenige' musst du aufpassen. *Much* und *little* verwendet man bei nicht zählbaren, *many* und *few* bei zählbaren Begriffen:

Beispiele: much – more – most   sugar
little – less – least   courage

many – more – most   cars
few – fewer – fewest   houses

- **Doppelte Steigerungsformen**: Einige Adjektive haben doppelte Steigerungsformen.

  Beispiele: **old**
  older – oldest   Who is <u>older</u>? Mr Waters or Mr Johnson?
  elder – eldest   He's the <u>eldest</u> in the family.
  (*elder* und *eldest* beziehen sich auf Familienmitglieder.)

  far
  farther – farthest   Our house is <u>farther/further</u> from the town centre.
  (Bei Entfernungen können beide Steigerungsformen verwendet werden.)

  further – furthest   I've got <u>further</u> information.

... rund ums Nomen: Adjektive

> **near**
> nearer – nearest   The <u>nearest</u> pub is at the corner of the street.
> *(nearer und nearest beziehen sich auf die Entfernung.)*
> nearer – next   We must get off at the <u>next</u> bus stop.
> *(next bezieht sich auf die Reihenfolge.)*
>
> **late**
> later – latest   We arrived <u>later</u> than we planned, but Katy was the <u>latest</u>.
> *(later bezieht sich auf die Zeit.)*
> latter – last   Tom and Bill are twins, the <u>latter</u> is 30 minutes younger than Tom.
> *(latter und last beziehen sich auf die Reihenfolge.)*
>
> **Beachte:** *Latest* kann auch ‚neuest/jüngst' heißen:
> *the latest fashion* = die neueste/jüngste Mode,
> aber: *last year's fashion* = die Mode des letzten/vergangenen Jahres

Aufgabe 3 Complete the sentences.

a) The success of Coca Cola was mainly due to the (größte) _____ publicity campaign the US had ever seen.

b) After having drunk Dr. Pemberton's medicine a few people were (gesünder) _____ than before.

c) The (das Erstaunlichste) _____ thing about its success is that Coke contains 99 % sugar water.

d) Today life is (geschäftiger) _____ than it used to be and people are (gestresster) _____.

e) The (das Wichtigste) _____ thing in big towns was the prohibition of alcohol.

f) Young capitalists became (hoffnungsvoller) _____ when they saw the success of companies like Ford, Woolworth, Coca Cola and so on.

g) When experimenting with the formula for Coke, Dr. Pemberton was (mehr Glück) _____ than his colleagues.

h) The customers were (zufriedener) _____ with carbonated water than with still water.

i) This was the (die schlaueste) _____ idea he ever had.

j) The chemist soon became one of the (der reichste) _____ men in Atlanta.

... rund ums Nomen: Adjektive 19

Aufgabe 4 Translate the following text into English.

Während des 2. Weltkrieges gab es in den USA oder in Europa nicht genug Zucker, deshalb rationierten ihn die Regierungen, d. h., die Leute konnten nicht so viel davon haben, wie sie wollten. Die schlimmsten Rationierungen waren die Zucker- und Benzinrationierungen. Amerikaner und Europäer mussten mit weniger Zucker auskommen, das hieß weniger Zuckerstücke oder Löffel Zucker für den Kaffee oder Tee. Die Firma Coca Cola war in einer schlimmen Lage, die sich noch verschlimmerte, als Kuba seine Zuckerexporte in die USA einschränkte. Es gelang den Direktoren von Coca Cola, die US Regierung davon zu überzeugen, dass Cola wichtig war für die Moral der Truppen, die im Ausland kämpften, und deshalb hatte die Firma die geringsten Zuckerrationierungen.

Aufgabe 5 Complete the sentences.

a) *near*

'Where's the _____ petrol station, please?'

'Where's the _____ petrol station, please?'

b) *late*

This is the _____ fashion in hairstyles.

These are his _____ hairs.

c) *late*

This is Ollie and Stan. The _____ always gets Ollie into trouble.

d) *little*

He's got _____ money.

He's got _____ money.

He's got the _____ money of all.

e) *far*

The town is _____ than they thought.

The youth hostel is _____.

f) *old*

Tom's brother is two years _____.

Tom's _____ brother is called Bob.

g) *bad*

On Monday the weather was _____.

On Sunday the weather was _____.

On Saturday the weather was _____.

Aufgabe 6 Put the adjectives in the *comparative* (comp.) or *superlative* (sup.).

In a safe at the Trust Company of Georgia, USA, lies the secret of the world's (popular, sup.) _____ soft drink. (little, comp.) _____ than half of the company directors are authorised to open the safe. It contains the (secret, sup.) _____ ingredients of Coca Cola. People have often attempted to discover the secret of Coca Cola's flavour, but the results were (little, comp.) _____ successful than expected.

The (famous, sup.) _____ chemical laboratories have discovered about 10 of the ingredients. In (far, comp.) _____ experiments in 1983, scientists found the ingredient 7X. It consists of several oils, but it has not yet been fully analyzed. A (far, comp.) _____ difficulty is finding the exact proportions of the ingredients. The proportion of the stimulant cocaine added to Coca Cola in its early stages became (little, comp.) _____ and _____ due to government regulations, and today the coca leaf extract 'cocaine' has been completely removed.

For those who want to reproduce the mixture, Coke contains:

sugar, caramel, caffeine, phosphoric acid (Phosphorsäure), cola-nut extract, citric acid (Zitronensäure), sodium (Natrium), lemon, orange, lime, glycerine, vanilla and nutmeg oil (Öl der Muskatnuss)

... rund ums Nomen: Adjektive

Aufgabe 7 a) Find the nouns corresponding to the adjectives.

long _length_ _____ broad _____ [e]

deep _____ [e] high _____ [aɪ]

wide _____ [i]

b) Find the adjectives corresponding to the nouns.

Estonia _____

Lithuania _____

Latvia _____

Czech Republic _____

Hungary _____

Cyprus _____

Malta _____

Poland _____

Der Bindestrich (hyphen)

Es gibt nur wenige, eindeutige Regeln für die Verwendung des Bindestrichs bei zusammengesetzten Wörtern. Dies gilt besonders für Zusammensetzungen, die aus zwei Nomen bestehen. So findet man z. B. *shoe shop* neben *shoe-shop* oder *lorry driver* neben *lorry-driver*. Im British English verwendet man den Bindestrich (mit wenigen Ausnahmen)

- bei Zusammensetzungen mit Adjektiv und einem Wort, das auf **-ed** oder **-ing** endet.
  Beispiele: blue-eyed, nice-looking, a fast-moving car
- bei Zusammensetzungen mit **co-, un-, ex-**.
  Beispiele: a German and American co-production, un-American, her ex-lover
- bei Zusammensetzungen mit Zahlwörtern und Wendungen, die ein Maß bezeichnen, wobei die Maßeinheit immer im Singular steht.
  Beispiele: a ten-minute pause, a three-hour walk, a two thousand-foot high mountain

---

Aufgabe 8 Use a hypen if necessary.

a) The ex President held a speech.
b) He was injured in a car crash.
c) The three hundred ton ship sank in the storm.
d) Is this fibre hand made?
e) Ask the waiter for a doggie bag.
f) I lost my credit card.

… rund ums Verb

3 Adverbien

Mit Adverbien werden einzelne Wörter oder Sätze in Bezug auf **Zeit, Raum, Art und Weise und Intensität** näher bestimmt. Während du das Adjektiv verwendest, um ein Nomen näher zu definieren (attributiver Gebrauch) oder um in Kombination mit einem Verb das Prädikat eines Satzes zu bilden (prädikativer Gebrauch), können sich Adverbien auf **Verben, Adjektive, andere Adverbien** oder auf einen ganzen **Satz** beziehen.

Beispiele: Peter worked quickly.
Sarah is extremely pretty.
The football team played fairly well.
Hopefully, you will pass the exam.

3.1 Formen der Adverbien

Wie wird das Adverb gebildet?

Man unterscheidet zwischen **ursprünglichen Adverbformen** (meistens Zeit- und Ortsadverbien wie *now, today, still, here, near, up*) und **Adverbien mit -ly**. Adverbien der Art und Weise werden häufig durch Hinzufügung von -ly an das jeweilige Adjektiv gebildet.

Beispiele: slow – slowly
equal – equally

- Bei Adverbien, die auf **-ly** gebildet werden, musst du folgende **Veränderungen der Schreibung** beachten: -y am Ende eines Adjektivs wird zu *-i;* *-e* am Ende eines Adjektivs bleibt vor *-ly* erhalten, Adjektive, die auf **Konsonant +-le** enden, erhalten ein *-y* anstelle des *-e*.

    Beispiele: happy – happily
    busy – busily
    aber: shy – shyly
    extreme – extremely
    dense – densely
    aber: true – truly, due – duly
    whole – wholly
    simple – simply
    gentle – gently
    probable – probably

- Adjektive, die auf *-ic* enden, erhalten als Adverbien die Endung *-ally*.
  Beispiele: fantast*ic* – fantastic*ally*
  bas*ic* – basic*ally*
  econom*ic* – economic*ally*
  aber: public – publicly
- Adjektive, die auf *-ll* enden, bilden das Adverb mit *-y*.
  Beispiele: fu*ll* – fully
  du*ll* – dully
- Das Adverb von *good* ist *well*.
  Beispiel: Tom is a <u>good</u> player – he plays <u>well</u>.
- Die Adjektive *friendly* und *silly* haben die Adverbformen *in a friendly way* und *in a silly way*.
  Beispiel: He looked at me in a <u>friendly way</u>.

Es gibt einige Adverbien, die in ihrer Bildung Besonderheiten aufweisen:
- **Adverbien mit den Formen von Adjektiven**
  Es gibt einige Adverbien, die die gleiche Form wie das entsprechende Adjektiv haben. Bei diesen Adverbien musst du besonders aufpassen: *fast, straight, early, extra, long, little, low* sowie *daily, weekly, monthly, yearly*.

Beispiele:	Adverb	Adjektiv
	The car goes <u>fast</u>.	He has got a <u>fast</u> car.
	We went <u>straight</u> home.	You must draw a <u>straight</u> line.
	He couldn't stay <u>long</u>.	It's a <u>long</u> way to Tipperary.
	The rolls cost <u>extra</u>.	I saved some <u>extra</u> money.
	The pilot flew <u>low</u>.	There is a <u>low</u> wall around the garden.
	This newspaper is published <u>weekly</u>.	The doctor makes a <u>weekly</u> visit.
	The parents' association of the school meets <u>monthly</u>.	Tom is at the <u>monthly</u> meeting of his club.

- **Adverbien mit zwei Formen**
  Einige Adverbien haben zwei Formen, die jedoch unterschiedliche Bedeutungen haben. Diese musst du auswendig lernen.

hard	hart	*hardly*	kaum
high	hoch	*highly*	höchst (im übertragenen Sinn)
free	umsonst	*freely*	frei
late	spät	*lately*	in jüngster Zeit
just	gerade	*justly*	gerecht
most	am meisten	*mostly*	meistens
fair	fair, anständig	*fairly*	ziemlich
close	nahe	*closely*	eng, dicht
near	nahe	*nearly*	beinahe, fast
pretty	ziemlich	*prettily*	hübsch

... rund ums Verb: Adverbien 25

Aufgabe 1 Holidaymakers in Europe: Complete the sentences with adjective or adverb.

A recent survey for a credit card company shows that it is the Germans who spend most money on travel. German holidaymakers spend nearly one third more than the British.

a) After the reunification of West and East Germany, the number of holidaymakers rose (drastic – drastically) _____.

b) (Actual – actually) _____ the Spanish spend most per head, which is surprising as Spain is (economic – economically) _____ weaker than Germany or Britain.

c) Germans visiting Britain are (high – highly) _____ interested in (historic – historically) _____ famous sights such as Stonehenge or the (busy – busily) _____ life in London's shopping-centres.

d) (Due – duly) _____ to the weather conditions, Germans do not enjoy staying in British seaside resorts such as Brighton. Compared to beaches in Italy or Spain, they consider the British seashore areas (dull – dully) _____.

e) British holidaymakers (most – mostly) _____ go to France on holiday. They are attracted (irresistible – irresistibly) _____ by the beaches of the Mediterranean. In August, (near – nearly) _____ every second car registration plate shows that the driver is British.

f) These days, holiday-making has become (increasing – increasingly) _____ expensive in Britain (due – duly) _____ to the strength of the British pound. The (typical – typically) _____ British bed and breakfast places demand (high – highly) _____ prices today. Still, it is always a pleasure for the tourist to be (hearty – heartily) _____ welcomed by the (gentle – gently) _____ landlady.

g) Lots of people travel to the Channel Islands Jersey and Guernsey for (economic – economically) _____ reasons: gold and silver jewellery are much cheaper there than in the rest of Europe. Moreover, people enjoy the (fantastic – fantastically) _____ prepared seafood and the clean beaches.

h) (Late – lately) _____ the banks of the Channel Islands have been attracting tourists who want to invest money without paying any taxes.

i) The transport between the Channel Islands is (main – mainly) _____ carried out by small planes seating eight to twelve passengers. The planes do not fly (high – highly) _____ above the sea, only at a height of 300 feet (about 100 metres). And these small planes are (absolute – absolutely) _____ safe: no accident has occurred for the last 50 years.

j) When Japanese or American holidaymakers travel to Europe, their trips are (whole – wholly) _____ organized by air companies offering package tours.

k) Italian tourist officials found out that the Japanese spend (most – mostly) _____ on souvenirs and luxury hotels. (Late – lately) _____ the Italian Ministry of Tourism declared (public – publicly) _____ that the Ministry preferred one Japanese tourist to two Americans or seven Germans. This statement caused (great – greatly) _____ anger among European holidaymakers. It can (hard – hardly) _____ be believed that this official statement is (serious – seriously) _____ because Italy needs the European holidaymakers' money (desperate – desperately) _____ .

Aufgabe 2 Getting to Know Britain – The South: Complete the sentences with the correct English expression.

The South of England extending from Kent to Cornwall is one of the (bekanntesten) _____ tourist areas of Great Britain. The South is not (intensiv) _____ industrialized. Kent is more (dicht) _____ populated than Cornwall. Cornwall is (im Wesentlichen) _____ an agricultural country, farming techniques are (hoch) _____ developed. In Cornwall (meistens) _____ cattle and sheep are reared. Nevertheless, Britain is (weitgehend) _____ dependent on imported food because Cornwall can not produce a (ausreichend) _____ amount of food. Kent attracts a (beträchtlich) _____ number of tourists because of its Roman and Norman sights. Today Dover and Folkestone are (geschäftig) _____ gateways to the Continent. Southampton is a major port offering (wöchentlich) _____ transatlantic crossings on big ocean liners. Here's a piece of advice for tourists: if you are interested in (reich) _____ decorated churches and castles, go to Kent. If you prefer swimming and sunbathing, go to the (schön) _____ situated Cornish seaside resorts.

Aufgabe 3 Mixed exercises: Fill in the correct word.

a) *late* oder *lately*:
   The bus arrived _____.
   Have you seen Peter _____?

b) *good* oder *well*:
   Did you do _____ in your test?
   Today I feel quite _____.
   She's a _____ cook.

c) *hard* oder *hardly*:
   All of you must work _____.
   He's lazy, he _____ works at all.
   Don't pull too _____.
   I could _____ understand the words.

d) *near* oder *nearly*:
   I _____ missed the bus.
   Don't go _____ the door.
   We are _____ ready.
   I've _____ finished.

e) *free* oder *freely*:
   Cigarettes are not _____ of customs duties.
   I _____ admit I was wrong.
   Peter always hides something, he never speaks _____.

3.2 Adjektiv oder Adverb nach bestimmten Verben

Bei welchen Verben darfst du keine Adverbien verwenden?

- Bei Verben, die einen **Zustand** oder eine **Eigenschaft** ausdrücken und die durch *be* ersetzt werden können, steht kein Adverb, sondern ein Adjektiv (= prädikativer Gebrauch). Verben dieser Art nennt man **Kopulaverben**. Zu ihnen gehören *seem, smell, feel, look, taste, sound, appear*.
  Beispiele: You look great today.
  Betty seems happy.
  This fish smells fresh.

- Wenn durch die Verben *look, feel, smell, sound, taste* jedoch eine **Tätigkeit** beschrieben wird, sie also nicht durch *be* ersetzt werden können, folgen keine Adjektive, sondern Adverbien.
  Beispiele: Peter looked at his little sister angrily.
  Smell this fish carefully, please. Is it all right?

- Wenn die Verben *appear, feel, look* einen **Gesundheitszustand** ausdrücken, so folgen keine Adjektive, sondern Adverbien.
  Beispiele: She was ill for a month, but she looks well now.
  After we had eaten the fish, we didn't feel well.
  Sandra does not appear well after the operation.

- Auf Verben, die eine **Veränderung eines Zustandes** ausdrücken, folgt kein Adverb, sondern ein Adjektiv (diese Verben werden im Deutschen zumeist mit ‚werden' wiedergegeben):
  Beispiele: The milk turned sour.
  The DJ became very popular.
  Dorothy always gets angry when she doesn't see a joke.
  The fans went crazy when their idol appeared.
  It began to grow dark.

Aufgabe 4 Paying compliments: Complete the sentences using adjective or adverb.

a) Oh, Mrs Waters, you're such a (gut) _____ cook. Your mulligatawny soup tastes (hervorragend) _____, it is always (fein) _____ seasoned with curry powder. I (besonders) _____ like your lamb chops, they smell (wunderbar) _____. Can I have some more?

b) Nelly you look (gut) _____ in your new Shetland wool pullover. It suits you very (gut) _____. May I feel the wool? It feels (wirklich weich) _____ _____. And the colour goes (unglaublich gut) _____ _____ with your brown hair. I must say you are the (hübscheste) _____ girl I know.

Aufgabe 5 Finding fault with somebody: Tell your friends what you don't like about them or what they should (not) do. The pictures and the words in brackets will help you.

a) You mustn't always forget _____
   _____
   (put – turn – sour)

b) Don't _____
   _____
   (behave – silly)

c) Don't _____
   _____
   (look – angry)

d) _____
   _____
   (look – more careful)

e) _____
   _____
   (sound – loud)

... rund ums Verb: Adverbien

f) _____
(smell – bad)

g) _____
(sound – silly)

h) _____
(not get furious – taste – not good)

i) _____
(look – untidy)

j) _____
(after all – want – get on – well)

3.3 Stellung der Adverbien im Satz

An welche Stelle im Satz stellst du das Adverb?

Adverbien können an verschiedenen Stellen im Satz stehen. Beachte jedoch die **Grundregel**: Das Adverb kann nicht zwischen dem Verb und seinem Objekt stehen. **Präge dir ein: a S a V O a** (a = Adverb, S = Subjekt, V = Verb, O = Objekt)

Beispiele: Hastily John ate his fish and chips.
John hastily ate his fish and chips.
John ate his fish and chips hastily.

- **Adverbien der Art und Weise** (*adverbs of manner*) wie *quickly, fast, in a silly way, hastily* stehen in der Regel **am Ende eines Satzes**.
  Beispiel: John answered the questions quickly.

- **Adverbien des Ortes und der Zeit** (*adverbs of place and time*) wie *here, there* und **adverbiale Bestimmungen des Ortes / der Zeit** wie *in the town centre, at the riverside, tomorrow, by now, next week* stehen ebenfalls meistens am **Ende eines Satzes**. Dabei gilt die **Grundregel: Ort vor Zeit**.
  Beispiele: The Potters live in the next house.
  We spent our holidays in the mountains.
  John telephoned us from Brighton yesterday.

  Enthält ein Satz zwei Adverbien der Zeit, so steht das Adverb, das eine kürzere Zeiteinheit bezeichnet, **vor** dem Adverb, das eine längere Zeiteinheit bezeichnet:
  Beispiel: I was in Scotland in August, 1998.

- **Satzadverbien**, also Adverbien, die einen ganzen Satz näher bestimmen (z. B. *unfortunately, luckily*), **stehen am Satzanfang**.
  Beispiel: Unfortunately, Mrs Potter had lost her car keys.

- **Häufigkeitsadverbien**, die eine **unbestimmte Häufigkeit** ausdrücken (*adverbs of indefinite frequency*) wie *always, never, ever, often, usually, regularly* stehen **zwischen Substantiv und Verb**. Adverbien, die eine **bestimmte Häufigkeit** ausdrücken (*adverbs of definite frequency*) wie *once, twice, three times, weekly, every two days* stehen meistens am **Ende eines Satzes**.
  Beispiele: John often visits us.
  I saw him once.

  sometimes kann am Anfang, in der Mitte oder am Ende des Satzes stehen.
  Beispiel: Sometimes Peter rings me up.
  Peter sometimes rings me up.
  Peter rings me up sometimes.

- In **Sätzen mit zusammengesetzten Zeiten** stehen die Adverbien meistens **nach dem ersten Hilfsverb**.
  Beispiel: He would certainly have told us.

... rund ums Verb: Adverbien

> - Wenn ein Satz **zwei oder drei Adverbien oder adverbiale Bestimmungen** enthält, so gilt die Grundregel **Ort vor Zeit** oder **Art und Weise vor Ort und vor Zeit**.
>   *Beispiele:* I'll leave <u>for London</u> <u>tomorrow</u>.
>   Peter sang <u>happily</u> <u>in the bathroom</u> <u>in the morning</u>.

Aufgabe 6 Immigrants: Rewrite the sentences and fill in the adverbs.

a) Phil has emigrated with his parents. *(recently – from Pakistan)*

b) He has been living … now. *(for two months – in Manchester)*

c) He speaks English, but at home he speaks Pakistani with his parents. *(well – often)*

d) He goes with them. *(often – at the weekends – to the cinema)*

e) One of his friends, Kim, is from Thailand. He arrived …, and he can speak English. *(hardly – a fortnight ago – only)*

f) Kim is interested in Kung Fu films. He has been to the cinema to see his favourite films. *(particularly – twice – since his arrival)*

g) Kim's parents could find a flat in Manchester. Kim's father complains that white British people find a flat. *(hardly – more easily)*

h) Though they come from different parts of the world, Phil and Kim are British subjects. *(oddly enough – too – completely)*

i) Prejudice against other races has been criticized. Britain is far from being a multi-racial society.
(often – severely – still – undoubtedly – in Britain – deeply rooted)

... rund ums Verb: Adverbien · 33

Aufgabe 7* Mixed exercise – The Cowboy hero: Write the sentences, completing them with the given words in the correct form.

Americans think that the cowboy symbolizes national virtues:

a) optimistic
   always
   The cowboys believe that good will triumph over evil.
   _____
   _____

b) never
   unfriendly
   He treats strangers …
   _____

c) hard
   tenacious
   always happy
   He works, he does his job, he is …
   _____
   _____

d) good
   in America
   immediately
   urgent
   rapid
   The cowboy became known after the Civil War when cattle were needed in the growing towns in the northern states.
   _____
   _____

e) radical
   In the 1890s the situation changed with the coming of the railroads and he was no longer used to drive cattle to the North.
   _____
   _____

f) original
   simple
   The cowboy was a farm labourer on horseback.
   _____

g) daily
   occasional
   The modern cowboy uses pickup trucks and helicopters to manage cattle all over the West.
   _____
   _____

h) relative
   probable
   There were few cowboys, not more than 50,000 in the United States during the cattle boom.
   _____
   _____

… rund ums Verb: Adverbien

i) hard
   near

   Nowadays it is known that two thirds of the cowboys were Blacks or Mexicans.
   _____
   _____
   _____

j) always
   frequently
   seldom
   main
   courageous

   In the cowboy myth, the cowboy is white and a southerner. He herds cattle, he rescues innocent girls and he fights bandits.
   _____
   _____
   _____

> ### Zusammensetzungen mit *all*
>
> - Vergleiche *already* (= schon) und *all ready* (= alle sind bereit/fertig):
>   *Beispiele:* already   I've already seen this film.
>   all ready   "Are you all ready?" – "No, Bob isn't."
> - Vergleiche *altogether* (= im Ganzen, insgesamt) und *all together* (= alle [zusammen]):
>   *Beispiele:* altogether   It rained sometimes, but altogether, the weather was bad.
>   all together   We went to the party all together.
>
> Weitere Zusammensetzungen:
>
> - *all-round* (= vielseitig begabt)
>   *Beispiele:* an all-round student/athlete/player, an all-rounder (= Allroundmann)
> - *all-star* (= mit berühmten (Film-/Theater-)Stars besetzt)
>   *Beispiel:* an all-star film
> - *all-in/all-inclusive* (= alles inbegriffen)
>   *Beispiel:* an all-in price

Aufgabe 8   Complete the sentences using expressions from above.

a) Come on, everybody sing. Let' sing _____.

b) "How much is it?" – "That's € 12 _____."

c) Are there extras or is it an _____ price?

d) My friend is an _____, he plays tennis, cricket and golf.

… rund ums Verb: Zeitformen des Verbs 35

4 Zeitformen des Verbs

Wie im Deutschen gibt es im Englischen drei Grundzeiten: *past* (Vergangenheit), *present* (Gegenwart) und *future* (Zukunft). Ein wesentlicher Unterschied ist jedoch folgender: Das Englische hat für jede Zeit **zwei Zeitformen** (*simple tense* und *progressive/continuous tense*). Damit werden verschiedene Aspekte einer Handlung ausgedrückt.

4.1 *present tense*

Die Zeitformen der Gegenwart sind im Englischen das *simple present* und das *present progressive*. Ihre jeweilige Verwendung unterliegt bestimmten Regeln.

Rund ums *simple present*

Wann verwendest du das *simple present*?

- Du verwendest das *simple present*, wenn du ausdrücken willst, dass eine Handlung **gewohnheitsmäßig, regelmäßig, oft** oder **nie** stattfindet.
  Signalwörter: *often, always, from time to time, every now and then, usually, every day, every week* usw.
  Beispiel: Peter visits us every Monday afternoon.

- Du gebrauchst das *simple present* bei Handlungen oder Tatsachen, die **allgemein gültig** oder **von längerer Dauer** sind. Hierzu gehören z. B. Fähigkeiten, Naturgesetze, Eigenschaften.
  Beispiele: The moon goes round the earth.
  The Queen reigns, but she does not rule.

- Du verwendest das *simple present*, wenn du eine **Handlungskette** beschreibst. Dies ist beispielsweise bei Berichten der Fall.
  Beispiel: The centre forward stops the ball, he turns round, shoots a goal.

- Du gebrauchst das *simple present* zum Ausdruck von **zukünftigen Handlungen in Nebensätzen** nach *if, unless, in case, when, whenever, till, as soon as, before, while*.
  Beispiel: If it rains, we'll stay at home.

- Du verwendest das *simple present* zum Ausdruck von **zukünftigen Handlungen, die fest geplant**, also Teil eines festgelegten Programms, eines Zeit- oder Fahrplans sind.
  Beispiel: School starts on September 16.

... rund ums Verb: Zeitformen des Verbs

Aufgabe 1 Complete the sentences with the correct verb form.

a) Wait till mother (kommen) _____.

b) When you (sein) _____ in hospital, we (besuchen) _____ you.

c) The Lord Mayor of London (eröffnen) _____ the exhibition tomorrow.

d) I (nicht leihen) _____ him this book unless he (zurückgeben) _____ me back my CDs.

e) He (abfahren) _____ at seven o'clock.

f) If (sein) _____ ill, I'll take this medicine.

g) He'll ring us up as soon as he (ankommen) _____.

h) She (feiern) _____ her birthday party on Friday.

i) If you (arbeiten) _____ hard, you'll succeed.

Rund ums *present progressive*

Wann verwendest du das *present progressive*?

- Du verwendest das *present progressive*, wenn du über eine Handlung sprichst, die zum Zeitpunkt des Sprechens **gerade stattfindet** und noch nicht abgeschlossen ist.
  Beispiel: At this moment he's working in the garden.

- Du verwendest das *present progressive* bei **geplanten Handlungen**, die in der Zukunft stattfinden sollen.
  Beispiel: I'm leaving on the 5.15 bus.

- Zusammen mit dem Adverb *always* drückt die Verlaufsform aus, dass etwas immer wieder geschieht, meist geht es um eine Handlung, die vom Sprecher missbilligt wird.
  Beispiel: You're always shouting at me.

Welche Verben darfst du nicht in die Verlaufsform setzen?

Es gibt einige Verben, die aufgrund ihrer Bedeutung nicht in der Verlaufsform stehen können. Diese Verben sind in ihrer Grundbedeutung **statisch** und können deswegen nicht in der dynamischen *progressive*-Form stehen.

- **Verben der Sinneswahrnehmung:** Die Verben *hear, see, smell, taste* werden in ihrer Grundbedeutung nicht in der Verlaufsform verwendet. Sie können zwar auch ins *present progressive* gesetzt werden, dann ändert sich jedoch ihre Bedeutung.
  Beispiele: The soup tastes of fish.
  I feel very cold.
  aber: Mother is tasting the soup. (Mutter probiert die Suppe.)
  The doctor is feeling Peter's broken leg. (Der Arzt tastet Peters gebrochenes Bein ab.)

- **Verben, die eine gefühlsmäßige Haltung ausdrücken:** *love, adore, like, dislike, prefer, mind, hate, detest, want, wish, desire, need* etc.
  Beispiel: Peter <u>likes</u> cornflakes for breakfast
- **Verben, die eine geistige Tätigkeit ausdrücken:** *know, think, doubt, suppose, hope, wonder, consider, understand, imagine, realize, remember* etc.
  Beispiel: I <u>think</u> Peter will come to the party.
- **Verben, die ein Besitzverhältnis oder einen Zustand ausdrücken:** *consist, possess, fit, belong, suit, concern, seem, contain* etc.
  Beispiel: This book <u>belongs</u> to the school library.
- **Das Verb *be*:** Als Zustandsverb kann *be* nicht in der Verlaufsform stehen. Wird das Verb in der *progressive form* verwendet, so ändert sich die Bedeutung. *be* drückt dann keinen allgemein gültigen Zustand aus, sondern bezieht sich auf vorübergehende Vorgänge oder Handlungen..
  Beispiele: He <u>is</u> a naughty boy.
  aber: The boy <u>is being</u> naughty. (Der Junge verhält sich (gerade) ungezogen.)

Aufgabe 2 *Simple present* or *present progressive?* Complete the sentences.

a) Do you know where your parents are at the moment?
   Yes, Mum (type) _____ a letter and Dad (clean) _____ the car.

b) This evening David (listen) _____ to Heavy Metal, the music is very loud.

c) Tom usually (work) _____ in the bank until 4, but today he (work) _____ until 6 o'clock.

d) Please can you tell me when the bus (leave) _____?

e) I (see) _____ that you (become) _____ impatient.

f) We (not go) _____ to the theatre very often, but when we (go) _____, we (enjoy) _____ it.

g) We (wait) _____ for our friends. They (know) _____ that we have to catch the train this morning.

h) He (want) _____ me to help him now.

i) I always (look forward) _____ to my holiday. This year I (look forward) _____ to going to Wales.

j) Helen (smoke) _____ a packet of cigarettes every day. Because she (prepare) _____ for her final examinations.

k) The buses (not run) _____ on Sundays, but this Sunday they (run) _____ to the city centre because of the President's visit.
l) My friend already (speak) _____ two languages, and now he (learn) _____ a third.
m) Look, Betty (talk) _____ to Kevin all the time, she (seem) _____ to like him.
n) I (like) _____ the smell of your aftershave. It (smell) _____ like peppermint.
o) No garlic salt on my chicken wings, please I (hate) _____ garlic.
p) I've got red wine and white wine. Which (you prefer) _____?
q) Where's Dave? – He (see) _____ Holly home.
r) I never (go) _____ by bus.
s) The lady (smell) _____ the perfumes, she (not know) _____ which one to buy.
t) Look, the guests (come) _____. Where's mum? – She's in the kitchen, she (taste) _____ the mulligatawny soup.
u) Where's Dave? – He (play) _____ with his computer, I (suppose) _____.
v) What (you think) _____ of your new neighbours? – I (consider) _____ them nice people.
w) Now I (wish) _____ that I hadn't told you that secret.
x) Oh, Betty, you (look) _____ nice in your new dress, it (suit) _____ you very well.
y) Whose car is this? – It (belong) _____ to Mr Waters.

Aufgabe 3 *Simple present* or *present progressive?* Complete the sentences.

a) *taste*

The ice cream _____ of bananas.

The chef _____ the soup.

b) smell

The girl _____ the rose.   The perfume _____ of roses.

Aufgabe 4 Mixed exercise: *Simple present* or *present progressive?* Complete the sentences.

Rudi is an exchange student from Germany at a college in a small town in Arkansas. He arrived a few days ago and found two new friends, Ann and David.

DAVID: Rudi, I (wonder) _____ if you (know) _____ our typical Saturday night entertainment – it's called cruising.
RUDI: Cruising? What's that?
ANN: Let's go cruising Saturday night. If you (come) _____ with us, you will see.

It's Saturday, seven thirty p.m., Rudi (wait) _____ for his new friends. Listen, a car (stop) _____ in front of the house where Rudi (live) _____ with his host family, the Foxes.

MRS FOX: Here's the key for the front door, Rudi. We won't be in when you (come) _____ home. We (visit) _____ our friends.

Now Rudi (get into) _____ David's car. David (rush) _____ off at full speed.

ANN: David, why (you drive) _____ so fast? You always (drive) _____ too fast.

DAVID: I never (drive) _____ too fast. Be quiet!

Rudi can hardly understand them, because the radio is so loud. Now the car (arrive) _____ at the main street of the town. Rudi is surprised: there are lots of cars full of teenagers. They (drive) _____ up and down the main street. The radios are on full blast and the boys and girls (shout) _____ at each other. There's a terrible noise.

DAVID: You see, Rudi, this is "cruising". On Saturday night, the main street is ours. (You like) _____ it?

RUDI: It's super. But I must say, I (feel) _____ hungry.

ANN: Okay, let's go to the Kentucky Fried Chicken drive-in.

The three youngsters (have) _____ a good time at the fast-food restaurant. David and Ann (fetch) _____ two soda drinks and a glass of beer for Rudi.

DAVID: You see, we never (drink) _____ alcohol when we are out with the car. We (not want) _____ to lose our driving licences.

Ann tells Rudi that they (spend) _____ most of their Saturday nights "cruising". Later in the evening, they usually (go) _____ to a cheap take-away for a hamburger or a pizza. And very often, Saturday night (end) _____ with a drive-in movie because it is much cheaper than a movie theatre.

ANN: Well, that's our way of relaxing and having some fun. I (hope) _____ you (like) _____ it.

RUDI: Not bad. But I (think) _____ I've drunk too much beer. Can you drive me home, please?

4.2 past tense

Das *simple past* und das *past progressive* sind Zeitformen der Vergangenheit.

Rund ums *simple past*

Wann verwendest du das *simple past*?

- Du verwendest das *simple past* bei Handlungen, die zu einem bestimmten Zeitpunkt oder in einem bestimmten Zeitraum der Vergangenheit abgeschlossen waren.
  Signalwörter: *yesterday, last week/year etc., two days/ weeks, etc. ago* etc.
  Im Deutschen verwendet man oft das Perfekt, wo im Englischen das *simple past* stehen muss.
  Beispiel: Yesterday I was at David's.
  Gestern bin ich bei David gewesen.
- Du verwendest das *simple past* auch bei **aufeinander folgenden Handlungen in der Vergangenheit**.
  Beispiel: We drove to a car park, got out, closed the windows and locked the doors.

Rund ums *past progressive*

Wann verwendest du das *past progressive*?

- Du verwendest das *past progressive* bei Handlungen, die zu einem bestimmten Zeitpunkt in der **Vergangenheit** gerade **im Verlauf**, also noch nicht abgeschlossen waren.
  Beispiel: Yesterday, at half past seven, we were playing a computer game.
- Du verwendest das *past progressive* auch bei Handlungen, die während eines **längeren Zeitraums** in der Vergangenheit stattfanden.
  Beispiel: Yesterday, from seven o'clock to half past seven, I was phoning my friend.
- Ebenso verwendest du das *past progressive* bei Handlungen, die **gleichzeitig** in der Vergangenheit stattfanden.
  Beispiel: They were singing happily while they were driving to the party.
- Das *past progressive* verwendet man auch bei **Rahmenhandlungen**, die im Hintergrund stattfanden, als plötzlich etwas anderes geschah.
  Beispiel: I was washing my hair, when the phone rang.

... rund ums Verb: Zeitformen des Verbs

Aufgabe 5 *Simple past* or *past progressive?* Complete the sentences.

a) I (want) _____ you to help me, but you (sleep) _____ so peacefully on the sofa that I (do) _____ the work alone.

b) I (look) _____ through my CDs and I (see) _____ that one (miss) _____.

c) I (have) _____ a bath while my mother (make) _____ breakfast.

d) The rain (begin) _____ at about two o'clock while we (drive) _____ to the beach.

e) When I (be) _____ in bed a mosquito (buzz) _____ around my head until I (manage) _____ to kill it.

f) Yesterday I (study) _____ from three o'clock to five o'clock.

g) Do you remember? On that day you (wear) _____ a blue dress which (suit) _____ you very well.

h) The child (look) _____ very frightened, she (scream) _____ all the time.

i) Before she (return) _____ to Germany she (work) _____ as an au pair with an American family from October to December.

j) The passengers (sleep) _____ until the stewardess (wake) _____ them up.

k) While we (fly) _____ over the Alps, a heavy storm (begin) _____.

l) The postman (walk) _____ past our house when suddenly our dog (jump) _____ at him and (tear) _____ his trousers.

m) While I (walk) _____ across the bridge the wind (blow) _____ off my cap.

n) The sun (shine) _____ when we arrived.

o) I (write) _____ postcards all afternoon.

p) Tom (break) _____ his leg while he (roller blade) _____.

q) The sun (set) _____ when we reached home.

r) Mr Thompson (work) _____ for an American firm in Serbia when the war (break) _____ out.

... rund ums Verb: Zeitformen des Verbs 43

Aufgabe 6   Complete the sentences.

a)

Yesterday the Thompsons _____ when _____.

b) Yesterday Peggy and Cathy _____ all day long.

c) Yesterday Tom _____.

d) Yesterday while Mrs Hicks _____, a thief _____ _____.

44 ... rund ums Verb: Zeitformen des Verbs

Aufgabe 7 Mixed exercise – Heavy metal coming to the fore: Complete the sentences with the correct verb form.

Some ten years ago heavy metal rock already (exist) _____, but few people (take) _____ notice of this new wave. Teenagers (love) _____ sweet, romantic songs that (make) _____ them dream. Music industry managers (show) _____ no interest. For several years heavy metal bands (play) _____ to small audiences in concert halls. In the early 90s things (change) _____.

A few months ago I (go) _____ to a concert by "The Chain Breakers", and I (cannot believe) _____ my eyes: a long queue of teenagers (wait) _____ in front of the concert hall, it (be) _____ "full house". For this special concert, most of the teenagers (wear) _____ leather clothes full of studs. Ears, noses, lips (be) _____ pierced. Once in the hall, the audience (scream) _____ outrageously until the concert (begin) _____.

The music I (listen) _____ to was rather monotonous, I (not understand) _____ the lyrics because the audience (make) _____ such a terrible noise all the time. When the concert was over, the fans (not leave) _____ the hall, they (wait) _____ for an encore. But the Chain Breakers (disappoint) _____ them.

A few days later, I (learn) _____ that the Chain Breakers (play) _____ from two to three o'clock in the morning on a music TV channel the following Saturday. Moreover, they (sell) _____ more and more recordings of their songs.

Why are these long-haired, heavy-metal bands with their tattooed biceps so successful? I think the reason is their wild, rebellious music.

4.3 *present perfect*

Das *present perfect* ist im Unterschied zum deutschen Perfekt keine reine Zeitform der Vergangenheit, sondern es drückt aus, dass eine **Handlung in der Vergangenheit begonnen hat und bis in die Gegenwart andauert** oder zumindest einen deutlichen Einfluss auf die Gegenwart ausübt.

Rund ums *present perfect simple*

Wann verwendest du das *present perfect simple*?

- Du verwendest das *present perfect simple* bei **Handlungen**, die vor dem Zeitpunkt des Sprechens, d. h. in der **Vergangenheit** begonnen haben und deren **Ergebnisse** jetzt, zum Zeitpunkt des Sprechens, vorliegen.
  Signalwörter: *now, just, today, this morning / week /month, still, ever, never, not yet, already, recently, lately, so far, up till now, since, for.*
  Beispiele: He <u>has put on</u> his thick pullover.
  (Ergebnis z. B.: He doesn't feel cold now.)
  <u>Have</u> you ever <u>met</u> Mr Thompson?
  (Ergebnis z. B.: Do you know Mr Thompson?)

- Du verwendest das *present perfect simple* auch bei Zuständen, die **vor dem Zeitpunkt des Sprechens** begannen und **jetzt** noch andauern.
  Beispiel: I <u>have had</u> a headache for two days. (My head is still aching now.)
  Im **Deutschen** steht hier das Präsens in Verbindung mit dem Zeitadverb ‚schon'. Dieses wird nicht übersetzt, da es in der Zeitform *present perfect* bereits enthalten ist:
  Beispiel: „Ich habe schon seit zwei Tagen Kopfweh."

- *since* **und** *for* **beim** *present perfect:* Das deutsche ‚seit' wird mit *since* wiedergegeben, wenn von dem Zeitpunkt die Rede ist, zu dem die Handlung begonnen hat. Mit *for* wird es wiedergegeben, wenn es um den Zeitraum geht, in dem etwas geschehen ist.
  Beispiele: She hasn't phoned me <u>since</u> last week.
  She hasn't phoned me <u>for</u> two days.

Aufgabe 8 Ask the following questions.

Du holst einen Austauschschüler am Flugplatz ab. Frage ihn,

a) ob er schon gefrühstückt hat.

b) ob er schon mehrmals geflogen ist.

c) ob er schon einmal in München war.

d) ob er den Reiseführer für München schon gelesen hat.

e) ob er seine Inlineskates mitgebracht hat.

Aufgabe 9 ASPCA in the US: Fill in *since* or *for*.

The ASPCA has been a protector of animals _____ 1866. They have made sure _____ more than a hundred years that people who are cruel to animals are punished. There have been laws to protect animals _____ the turn of the century. The ASPCA has had its own animal shelters and hospitals _____ at least 50 years. _____ the second half of the 19th century no less than 500 societies like ASPCA have been founded, which shows the Americans' love of pets.

Aufgabe 10 Enough food? Fill in *since* or *for* and complete the sentences with the correct verb form.

a) There (not be) _____ a famine in England _____ the Middle Ages.

b) In some African regions, it (not rain) _____ years, and the people (not have) _____ enough food _____ over a year.

c) A recent health report says that Americans (eat) _____ too much protein from meat, cheese and eggs _____ the war.

d) The Kellogg Foundation, founded by the inventor of Kelloggs' cornflakes (advise) _____ Americans to eat less meat _____ 1930. _____ that time the number of vegetarians (rise) _____ considerably.

e) On the other hand: about four million children (not have) _____ enough food to eat their fill _____ the day they were born.

Rund ums *present perfect progressive*

Wann verwendest du das *present perfect progressive*?

- Die Verlaufsform des *present perfect* verwendest du bei Handlungen und Zuständen, die in der **Vergangenheit begannen** und in der **Gegenwart und** meistens auch in der **Zukunft noch andauern**. Während die *simple*-Form des *present perfect* vor allem das Resultat einer Handlung betont, benutzt du die Verlaufsform, um die Tätigkeit an sich in den Mittelpunkt zu stellen.
  Beispiel: I have been writing letters all morning. (= Ich schreibe jetzt immer noch.
    Die Tätigkeit ist wichtig, nicht die Anzahl der Briefe.)
  aber: I have written three letters. (= Ich bin soeben damit fertig geworden.
    Die Briefe können jetzt abgeschickt werden.)

- Verben, die **eher Zustände als Handlungen ausdrücken**, stehen meistens in der Verlaufsform des *present perfect*. Die wichtigsten dieser Verben sind *lie, stay, wait, sit, study, learn, live, rest*.
  Beispiel: She has been lying in bed all day long.

- Häufig findet sich das *present perfect progressive* **nach *all* mit Zeitangabe** (*all morning, all this year* etc.) sowie **nach *since* und *for***.
  Beispiele: I have been studying all morning.
    I have been playing the piano since 9 o'clock.

  Ebenso wie für das *present progressive* gilt, dass einige Verben nicht in der Verlaufsform des *present perfect* stehen können, z. B. *see, hear, notice, smell, taste, believe, feel, think, know, understand, remember, forget, want, wish, love, like, dislike, seem, appear, belong to, consist of, possess, own, matter, contain*.

- Du verwendest das *present perfect progressive* bei Handlungen, die in der **Vergangenheit** stattfanden, die aber durch einen **„unerwünschten Nebeneffekt"** noch Auswirkungen auf die **Gegenwart** haben.
  Beispiel: You're all dirty. Have you been playing in the garden?

Aufgabe 11 Complete the sentences with the correct verb form.
a) Who (lock) _____ the door?
b) I (never see) _____ such an animal.
c) They (live) _____ here since 1990.
d) I (look) _____ at this photo for ten minutes, but I can't see her on it.
e) We (wait) _____ in the rain for half an hour.
f) I (know) _____ him for several years.
g) The cat (sit) _____ in my armchair all evening.
h) I feel dizzy, I think I (play) _____ computer-games too long.
i) I (not hear) _____ from you for a long time.

j) We (ring) _____ the bell for five minutes, but nobody has opened the door.
k) My brother (study) _____ sociology for three years now.
l) I (always hate) _____ that kind of job.
m) How long (you learn) _____ English?
n) Nobody (knock) _____ at the door since I have been back.
o) I (relax) _____ in the garden all afternoon.

Aufgabe 12 Complete the sentences with the correct verb form.

a) "Who (eat) _____ from my plate?"

b) "You look exhausted."
"Yes, I (work) _____ in the garden."

c) "The window was okay a moment ago. (Play) _____ football in the yard?"

d) "Oh dear, I'm red all over. I (lie) _____ in the sun too long."

e) "The tablecloth is full of stains. (Play) _____ with your food?"

Aufgabe 13 Stan Laurel and Oliver Hardy: *Simple Past, present perfect* or *present perfect progressive?*

Stan Laurel and Oliver Hardy made their finest films in the 20s and 30s, yet their popularity (continue) _____ to grow ever since. Recently the United States Postal Office (issue) _____ a commemorative stamp; this year the current owner of the film rights (licence) _____ the films to cable television where they appear each week and lately there (be) _____ an all-day "marathon" festival on the screen.

Over the years many writers (analyse) _____ the team's astonishing success. They (not find) _____ the answer to the question yet. Why (remain) _____ Stan and Ollie so popular to this day? L & H fans (see) _____ their films dozens of times, and every time they (laugh) _____ at the gags again and again throughout the films.

One critic wrote: The central theme behind their gags is "friendship". Stan is unable to perform even the simplest tasks, Ollie is always angry with him, but their friendship is constant, they always care for each other. It is probable that this "friendship" (attract) _____ movie-goers up to this day.

4.4 *past perfect*

> Das *past perfect* ist die Zeitform der Vorvergangenheit. Auch für diese Zeitstufe gibt es eine *simple*- und eine *progressive*-Form.

Rund ums *past perfect simple*

> **Wann verwendest du das *past perfect simple*?**
> - Das *past perfect* verwendest du bei Handlungen und Zuständen, die **vor** einem bestimmten Zeitpunkt in der **Vergangenheit** bereits **abgeschlossen** waren.
>   *Beispiel:*   Yesterday at two o'clock I had had dinner.
>   (= Mein Essen war gestern um zwei Uhr bereits zu Ende.)
>   *aber:* Yesterday at two o'clock I had dinner.
>   (= Mein Essen begann gestern um zwei Uhr.)
> - Oft wird das *past perfect* benutzt, um die **Reihenfolge** zu verdeutlichen, in der Handlungen stattgefunden haben. Der Vorgang, der zu einem früheren Zeitpunkt stattgefunden hat, steht im *past perfect*, während das spätere, darauf folgende Geschehen durch das *simple past* ausgedrückt wird.
>   *Beispiel:*   After the bell had rung, the children left the classroom.

Aufgabe 14   Complete the sentences with the correct verb form.
a) Yesterday my friend (arrive) _____ at the station.
b) I (not expect) _____ him, because he (say) _____ that he would arrive one day later.
c) He (be able) _____ to finish his work earlier and he (take) _____ the next train.
d) He (even have) _____ time to buy a present for me before the train (leave) _____.
e) He (give) _____ it to me. It (be) _____ a small ivory elephant and I (be) _____ delighted with it.

... rund ums Verb: Zeitformen des Verbs 51

Aufgabe 15   Stan and Ollie: Complete the sentences with the correct verb form.

Stan, whose real name (be) _____ Arthur Stanley Jefferson, (be) _____ born in 1890 in a small town in Lancashire, England. His father (run) _____ a theatre and as a child, Stan (often watch) _____ the comedians on the stage. By the time he was eight, he (already learn) _____ a lot of their jokes and gags.
At the age of 16, he (already write) _____ a bloodthirsty melodrama which, however, (be not) _____ a success. Before he (begin) _____ to work with Ollie, he (act) _____ in short films – most of which were flops. His breakthrough (come) _____ with his film partner Ollie.
Born in 1892 in Harlem, Georgia, Ollie's full name (be) _____ Oliver Norvell Hardy. His mother encouraged his interest in singing, and in 1900 the boy (already tour) _____ the Southern states as a choir boy. He (like) _____ all kinds of instruments, especially the drums. In his early films he sometimes plays the drums which he (learn) _____ in a Military College. In his early films he (fail) _____ badly, but things (change) _____ when Stan, the right partner, (come) _____ along.
Gilbert Anderson, an actor who (play) _____ in the first American Western "The Great Train Robbery" in 1903 and who (found) _____ a film company (engage) _____ Stan and Ollie in 1915. This (mean) _____ the beginning of a world career for the two completely different characters.

Rund ums *past perfect progressive*

> **Wann verwendest du das *past perfect progressive*?**
> - Diese Zeit verwendest du bei Handlungen, die zu einem bestimmten Zeitpunkt in der **Vergangenheit noch nicht abgeschlossen** waren.
>   *Beispiel:* Peter was tired because he had been working at McDonald's since five o'clock. (= Er arbeitete auch nach 5 Uhr noch weiter.)
> - Mit dem *past perfect progressive* betonst du vor allem die **Tätigkeit an sich**, während die *simple*-Form des *past perfect* das Ergebnis einer Handlung in den Mittelpunkt stellt.
>   *Beispiel:* Sarah's right hand hurt, because she had been writing letters all morning.
>   *aber:* Sarah went to the letter-box because she had written three letters.

Aufgabe 16 Elvis Presley: Complete the sentences with the correct verb form.

Before Elvis Presley, the most renowned American singers (be) _____ Frank Sinatra, Bing Crosby and Dean Martin; Elvis, however, outrivalled them all. He (never dream) _____ of becoming a singer. He came from a poor family. After Elvis (leave) _____ high school, he found a job as a lorry driver. He (work) _____ for two years when he recorded "That's All Right, Mama", originally a blues song. He soon (be) _____ number one on the world list of singers.

After he (record) _____ songs for 20 years, he was a multimillionaire. Before he did his military service in 1958, he (start) _____ a cultural and sexual revolution in the heads of the American youth.

Since 1959 the sales of his records (rise) _____, when his wife, Priscilla and his daughter Lisa left him. After the divorce Elvis could not overcome his loneliness. He began to drink. After he (take) _____ drugs for several years, he died of a heart attack in 1977, only 41 years old. After his death Elvis Presley became a myth and even today half a million people visit his grave every year.

4.5 *future tense*

> Das *future tense* ist die Zeitform der Zukunft. Wie bei den anderen Zeitformen kennt das Englische auch für das *future tense* eine *simple-* und eine *progressive*-Form. Neben dem *will-future* gibt es zudem das so genannte *going-to-future*. Zukünftiges Geschehen kann jedoch teilweise auch mithilfe von anderen Zeitformen ausgedrückt werden.

... rund ums Verb: Zeitformen des Verbs 53

> **Welche Möglichkeiten hast du, um zukünftige Handlungen auszudrücken?**
>
> - *going-to-future:* Zukünftige Handlungen werden mit *going to* ausgedrückt, wenn jemand die feste **Absicht** hat, etwas zu tun. *going to* verwendest du ebenso, wenn eine zukünftige Handlung unvermeidlich eintreten wird und wenn dies schon in der Gegenwart zu erkennen ist.
>   *Beispiele:* John <u>is going to leave</u> tomorrow.
>   It <u>is going to rain</u>. (z. B.: Der Himmel ist bereits voller Regenwolken.)
>
> - **will-future:** Zukünftige Handlungen werden mit *will* ausgedrückt, wenn sie auch ohne Absicht oder Zutun des Sprechers mit Sicherheit eintreten werden. *will* drückt also eine **neutrale Vorhersage** aus. *will* verwendet man außerdem, wenn man vermutet, dass eine Handlung eintreten wird.
>   *Beispiele:* My birthday <u>will be</u> on a Friday.
>   The weather <u>will be</u> fine tomorrow.
>
> - **Verlaufsform des *will-future*:** Handlungen, die zu einem bestimmten Zeitpunkt oder während eines Zeitraums in der Zukunft gerade **im Verlauf** sein werden, drückst du mit der Verlaufsform des *will-future* aus.
>   *Beispiel:* This time next week I <u>will be visiting</u> smugglers' holes in Cornwall.
>
> - **Futur II:** Bei Handlungen, die zu einem Zeitpunkt **in der Zukunft** bereits **abgeschlossen** sind, verwendest du das Futur II.
>   *Beispiel:* I hope they <u>will have found</u> accomodation before night comes.
>
> - Zukünftiges Geschehen kannst du auch durch **andere Zeitformen** ausdrücken. Geplante Handlungen werden oft durch das *present progressive* ausgedrückt, während Handlungen, die durch einen Zeitplan festgelegt sind, meist im *simple present* stehen (siehe 4.1).

Aufgabe 17 Complete the sentences with the correct verb form.

a) I (buy) _____ new tyres for my mountain bike, the old ones are worn out. I (buy) _____ them when I have enough money.

b) Look, the swallows are flying low, I'm sure it (rain) _____, let's hurry up, or we (get) _____ wet.

c) You never give me back my money. I (not lend) _____ you money anymore.

... rund ums Verb: Zeitformen des Verbs

Aufgabe 18 Plans for holidays: Use *going-to* or *will* where appropriate.

Erzähle deinem Freund/deiner Freundin aus England,
a) dass du dieses Jahr die Absicht hast, deine Ferien in Cornwall zu verbringen.
b) dass du demnächst die Überfahrt von Cherbourg nach Weymouth buchen wirst.
c) dass du fest vorhast, Land's End und einige Zinnminen zu besichtigen.

Frage ihn/sie,
d) ob dort viele Touristen sein werden.
e) ob es freie Zimmer in Privathäusern geben wird.
f) ob er/sie glaubt, dass es im August viel regnen wird.

Aufgabe 19 Plans for Cornwall: What will these people be doing when they are in Cornwall next week? Write full sentences.

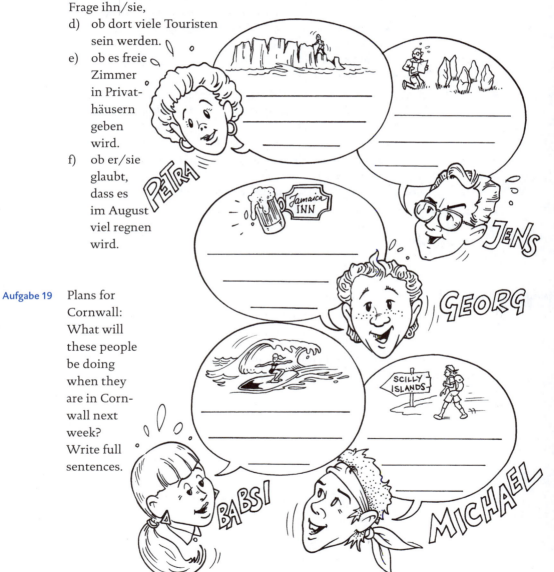

Aufgabe 20 Activities in Cornwall: Use the correct verb form.

Die fünf Urlauber in Cornwall erzählen ihren englischen Freunden, was sie am Ende ihres Urlaubs alles erlebt haben werden.

a) Petra wird auf Dutzende von Klippen geklettert sein.

___

b) Jens wird viele keltische Opferstätten fotografiert haben.

___

c) Georg wird in einem typischen Pub in Cornwall sein Bier getrunken haben.

___

d) Babsi wird gelernt haben, wie man auf dem Atlantik surft.

___

e) Michael wird das tropische Museum auf den Scilly-Inseln besucht haben.

___

Aufgabe 21* Mixed exercise – Agatha Christie's "The Mousetrap": Complete with the correct verb forms.

"The Mousetrap" (be) _____ the world's longest running play. Peter Saunders first (present) _____ it in 1952 at the St Martin's Theatre in London. It (be) _____ 50 years old in 2002. The play (open) _____ on 25th November 1952. Since the opening night, more than 10 million people (see) _____ the play, and more than 250 actors (appear) _____ on the stage. Seven years after Hitler's death in 1945, "The Mousetrap" (open) _____. By 1992 a lot of authors (translate) _____ the play into 24 languages. Today, theatre-goers in 44 different countries (can see) _____ the play.

... rund ums Verb: Zeitformen des Verbs

Peter Saunders still (own) _____ the rights of the play which film companies (try) _____ to buy for years. He says: "I (not allow) _____ a film company to make a film as long as "The Mousetrap" (run) _____ in a London theatre."

Aufgabe 22* Mixed exercise – Our changing world: Use the correct verb form.

The Earth (have) _____ a limited amount of oil and coal, wood and soil. For centuries people (use up) _____ these natural resources.
The consequences are: the deserts of the world (grow) _____ bigger and bigger. Water and air pollution (kill) _____ more and more plants and animals every year. Experts say that it (not be) _____ safe to swim in rivers and lakes in the years to come. Every year people (cut down) _____ forests the size of Britain. By the year 2015 one third of all the tropical forests (destroy) _____.
The exhaust fumes from cars, buses and trucks (keep) _____ poisoning the air. At present, Germany's Black Forest (die) _____. All forests (disappear) _____ by the year 2030? It is our children and grandchildren who (live) _____ on an Earth that generations (ruin) _____ for centuries. It is up to us to save the Earth before it (be) _____ too late.

Aufgabe 23 Make the following verbs negative by adding *un-* or *dis-*.

appear	_____	trust	_____
load	_____	continue	_____
do	_____	agree	_____
block	_____	plug	_____
approve	_____	obey	_____

Die Endungen *-ise* und *-ize*

Im British English werden die meisten Verben nur mit *-ise* geschrieben: *surprise, exercise, improvise, televise, advertise, advise, comprise, despise, analyse* usw. Folgende Verben können im British English sowohl mit *-ise* als auch mit *-ize* geschrieben werden: *realise/realize, sympathise/sympathize, computerise/computerize, baptise/baptize*.
Im American English ist die Schreibung mit *-ize* häufiger.

5 Passiv

Aktivsätze und Passivsätze unterscheiden sich wesentlich darin, aus welcher Perspektive man eine Handlung sieht.

- Im **Aktivsatz** wird der **Ausführende der Handlung (= Agens)** als wichtig empfunden, er steht am Anfang.
  Beispiel: The police arrested the pickpocket.
  (= Die Polizei und nicht etwa der Bestohlene oder Passanten nahmen den Taschendieb fest.)

- Im **Passivsatz** wird **die von der Handlung betroffene Person oder Sache (= Patiens)** als wichtiger empfunden.
  Beispiel: The pickpocket was arrested (by the police).
  (= Der Taschendieb wurde festgenommen. Der Ausführende der Handlung ist hier weniger wichtig.)

Passivsätze verwendest du also dann, wenn derjenige, der die Handlung ausführt, **unwichtig, unbekannt** oder so **selbstverständlich** ist, dass er nicht genannt werden muss.

Beispiele: This dangerous mountain is seldom climbed.
The shop was broken into.
The theatre was booked out when we arrived.

5.1 Formen des Passivs

Wie bildest du das Passiv?

Zu jeder Zeitform des Verbs gibt es auch eine Passivform.

- Die *simple*-Formen im Passiv
  Jeweilige Form von *to be* + *past participle*

tense	active	passive
simple present	He writes a letter.	A letter is written (by him).
simple past	He wrote …	… was written …
present perfect	He has written …	… has been written …
past perfect	He had written …	… had been written …
future	He will write …	… will be written …
conditional	He would write …	… would be written …
future + conditional	He will/would have written …	… will/would have been written …
gerund	I remember him writing …	I remember a letter being written …
auxiliary + infinitive	He ought to write …	… ought to be written …

... rund ums Verb: Passiv

> - **Die *progressive*-Formen des Passivs** kommt relativ selten vor. Gebildet werden sie mit der jeweiligen *progressive*-Form von *be + being + past participle*.
>   *Beispiel:*   The car <u>is being repaired</u>.
> - Der **Urheber der Handlung**, also das Agens, kann auch in Passivsätzen erwähnt werden. Wenn die Ursache oder der Verursacher wichtig erscheint, wird eine Präpositionalphrase mit *by* angeschlossen.
>   *Beispiel:*   This poem <u>was written</u> <u>by Shakespeare</u>.

Aufgabe 1   The plane takes off …: Write sentences in the passive voice using the following words: *to weigh the luggage, to announce the flight, to control the hand luggage, to give someone the boarding card, to show someone one's seat on the plane*

a) On Friday Mr Thompson flies to New York.
Before the plane takes off,   Mr Thompson's luggage is _____.
the flight _____.
his _____.
the boarding card _____ to him.
his _____.

b) Next weekend Mr Hedges will fly to San Francisco.
Before the plane takes off,   Mr Hedge's luggage will _____.
the flight _____.
his _____.
the boarding card _____.
his _____.

c) Last weekend Mr Benson flew to Atlanta.
Before the plane took off,   Mr Benson's luggage _____.
the flight _____.
his _____.
the boarding card _____.
his _____.

d) This time tomorrow Mr Jones will have taken off.
Before take-off,   Mr Jones' luggage will _____.
the flight _____.
his _____.
the boarding card _____.
his _____.

e) Poor Mr Bethman. He wanted to go to Los Angeles but his flight was cancelled at the last minute because of bad weather conditions.
Before the flight was cancelled, Mr Bethman's luggage had _____.
                          the flight _____.
                          his _____.
                          the boarding card _____.
                          his _____.

Aufgabe 2   Translate these sentences into German.

a) The safe had been carefully locked.

b) Last night it was forced open by burglars.

c) All the money was stolen.

d) Up to now no finger prints have been detected.

e) Will the burglars ever be caught?

f) The burglars would be caught if Sherlock Holmes took over the case.

g) The safe would not have been forced open if the alarm system had not been out of order.

h) At last the burglars were arrested because Inspector Columbo had been given the case.

5.2 Verschiedene Arten von Passivsätzen

Rund um das persönliche und unpersönliche Passiv bei Verben des Denkens und Meinens

Welche Arten von Passivsätzen kannst du mit Verben wie *know, say, believe* usw. bilden?

Grundsätzlich kannst du mit Verben des Denkens und Meinens im Englischen zwei Arten von Passivsätzen bilden. Neben dem „unpersönlichen Passiv", das im Deutschen die einzige Möglichkeit ist, kann im Englischen auch ein „persönliches Passiv" gebildet werden. „Persönlich" wird diese Art von Passivsätzen genannt, weil das Subjekt des Passivsatzes eine Person und keine Sache ist.

- **unpersönliche Passivsätze**
  Beispiel: It is known that Mr Thompson is a careful driver.

- **persönliche Passivsätze**
  Dabei wird an die persönliche Passivkonstruktion ein *to*-Infinitiv angeschlossen. Das persönliche Passiv steht nach den Verben *think, believe, suppose, consider, expect, know, say, report*. Diese Art von Passivsätzen gibt es im Deutschen nicht. Wenn man Sätze mit persönlichem Passiv ins Deutsche übersetzt, muss man Hilfskonstruktionen wie ‚angeblich, man sagt, soll' verwenden.

  Beispiele: Mr Thompson is known to be a careful driver.
  He is believed to drive slowly when the roads are icy.
  The boy is said to be badly injured.
  Angeblich ist der Junge schwer verletzt.
  Der Junge soll schwer verletzt sein.
  Man sagt, der Junge sei schwer verletzt.

Aufgabe 3 Family problems: Form sentences using a personal construction in the passive voice.

a) People say that many parents have too little time for their children.

b) It is said that quite a lot of fathers spend more time watching football on TV than talking to their children.

c) We know that children need their parents' time and love.

d) People often criticize mothers for taking up employment instead of caring for their families.

e) It is often wrongly considered that single parents are incapable of raising children.

f) Some people expect the state to compensate for the lack of attention to children by providing more nursery schools.

Aufgabe 4 America and the Native Americans: Put the sentences into the passive voice.

a) The Whites defeated the Indians.

b) They almost wiped them out.

c) They took away their land.

d) They had broken all the treaties with the Indians.

e) They had driven them into areas with infertile soil.

f) They called these areas reservations.

g) They said that the Indians were an inferior race.

h) They knew that the Indians were brave fighters.

i) Today the Americans help the Native Americans.

j) They will give them land with fertile soil.

k) They have already organized better education for them.

l) They care for their health.

m) They often help them to build up a tourist industry.

n) They have given them civil rights.

Rund um das Passiv bei Verben mit direktem und indirektem Objekt

Wie bildest du das Passiv bei Verben mit zwei Objekten?

Bei Verben mit zwei Objekten kannst du **zwei Arten von Passivsätzen** bilden. Eine Möglichkeit besteht darin, das indirekte Objekt des Aktivsatzes zum Subjekt des Passivsatzes zu machen (Passivsatz 1). Bei der zweiten Möglichkeit wird das direkte Objekt des Aktivsatzes zum Subjekt des Passivsatzes gemacht (Passivsatz 2). Das indirekte Objekt wird in diesem Fall mit to angeschlossen.

Beispiele: They promised Alan a new computer.
Alan was promised a new computer. (Passivsatz 1)
A new computer was promised to Alan. (Passivsatz 2)

Passivsätze, bei denen die Handlung auf eine Person bezogen ist (persönliches Passiv, siehe Satz 1), sind wesentlich häufiger als Passivsätze, bei denen eine Sache im Mittelpunkt steht (Satz 2). Die häufigsten Verben, die zwei Objekte zu sich nehmen können, sind *promise, give, send, teach, show, lend, allow, ask, tell, call, offer, refuse, pay, deny, answer, appoint.*

Beispiele: He had been offered a good job.
A good job had been offered to him.

Aufgabe 5 Race problems in South Africa: Write two sentences in the passive voice.
Before apartheid was abolished, the black population suffered from injustice.

a) The whites did not give the coloured people the right to vote.
   The coloured people were not given the right to vote.
   The right to vote was not given to the coloured people.

b) The whites paid them low wages.

c) The whites constantly showed them their inferiority.

d) The whites denied the Blacks equal job opportunities.

e) The whites gave the underprivileged shabby houseing in the Homelands.

f) They promised the coloured population improvements that were never realized.

g) They taught the blacks absolute obedience.

h) In the end, the white government had to give freedom to Nelson Mandela, who broke the whites' power.

Rund um die Stellung der Präpositionen und Verbpartikel in Passivsätzen

Wenn Präpositional- oder Partikelverben wie *to look at, to explain to, to take out, to bring up* ins Passiv gesetzt werden, steht die Präposition oder die Verbpartikel direkt nach dem Verb. Vergleiche:

Aktiv	Passiv
He looked at the picture.	The picture was looked at.
A car ran over the cat.	The cat was run over (by a car).
They will lock up the house before they leave.	The house will be locked up before they leave.
His aunt brought him up.	He was brought up by his aunt

Aufgabe 6 Put the sentences into the passive voice.

a) Our neighbour looked after our pets.

b) We looked for the key everywhere.

c) We must look into this matter more carefully.

d) You can look up these words in a dictionary.

e) They switched on the radio.

f) Someone had broken into the house.

g) They will call for a specialist.

h) What do they use this tool for?

i) They called off the match because of the rain.

j) They put away the dishes 10 minutes ago.

Aufgabe 7* Mixed exercise – "Give Fish a Break": Complete the sentences with the correct verb form.

a) Environmentalists are alarmed, because in recent years the ocean (ist überfischt worden) _____.

b) The underwater ecosystems (werden zur Zeit bedroht) _____ by the Japanese fishing float.

c) If a big tuna (wird gefangen) _____, it (wird verkauft) _____ for about $ 60,000 in Japan.

d) Fishermen (sind motiviert worden) _____ by these profits.

e) Shark fins (werden zur Zeit bestellt) _____ by Chinese restaurants in growing quantities as they (werden betrachtet) _____ a speciality.

f) It is doubtful whether the shark (kann gerettet werden) _____.

g) A WWF (World Wildlife Fund) conservation programme for whales, sea cows, dolphins and turtles (ist nicht unterstützt worden) _____ by China, Japan and Norway.

h) WWF is trying to convince fishermen that more money (kann verdient werden) _____ by whale-watching tourism than by dead whales.

i) The first positive results (können gesehen werden) _____: in more and more American restaurants swordfish (ist aus den Speisekarten genommen worden) _____ out of the menus, because young swordfish (werden zur Zeit gefangen) _____ before they are old enough to reproduce.

j) The managers of these restaurants agree: the swordfish (muss gegeben werden) _____ a chance.

k) These restaurants (werden belohnt) _____ by the WWF: The logo of "WWF", the Panda bear (kann benutzt werden) _____ free of charge in advertisements by these restaurants.

... rund ums Verb: Passiv

Aufgabe 8* Mixed exercise: Margaret Sanger – Pioneer of Women's Liberation. Read the following text and then complete the sentences with the information given in the text. Use passive sentences.

People know Margaret Sanger as the woman who legalized birth control. She was born into an Irish working-class family in Corning, N.Y., in 1879. As a young girl doctors had trained her to be a nurse and a midwife in the poorest neighbourhoods of New York City. In her fight for birth control she wrote articles in newspapers called "What Every Girl Should Know". The state imprisoned her repeatedly for writing what it regarded as obscene articles. When she had founded the American birth control league she was able to help thousands of women. Her work extended as far as India. Fewer young girls became pregnant because she introduced sex education into schools. She informed mothers with more than nine children about family planning. After the Second World War European countries adopted her social work for women. Margaret Sanger is said to be the most influential pioneer of sexual equality in the 20th century.

a) _____ as the woman who legalized birth control.

b) She could help sick people and pregnant women because _____ _____.

c) _____ repeatedly by the state for writing obscene articles.

d) _____ by her, she was able to help thousands of women.

e) Fewer young girls became pregnant, because _____ into schools by her.

f) Mothers with more than nine children _____ by her _____.

g) After the Second World War _____ by European countries.

> **Zusammensetzungen** *(compounds)*
> Zusammensetzungen werden meistens mit einem Bindestrich geschrieben.
> *Beispiel:* home-made (= selbst gemacht).

Aufgabe 9 Find the compounds.

schneebedeckt	a _____	mountain
handgestrickt (to knit)	a _____	pullover
mit langen Haaren	a _____	boy
gut angezogen	a _____	lady
gut gemeint	a _____	plan
egozentrisch	a _____	person
selbstbeherrscht	a _____	character
selbstständig	a _____	businessman

> **Verdoppelung von Endkonsonanten beim Anhängen einer Endung, die mit einem Vokal beginnt**
> - Bei einsilbigen Wörtern wird der Endkonsonant beim Anfügen einer Endung verdoppelt, wenn dem Endkonsonanten ein kurzer Vokal vorausgeht.
>   *Beispiel:* hop – hopping   aber: hope – hoping
> - Bei mehrsilbigen Wörtern wird der Endkonsonant nur dann verdoppelt, wenn das Wort auf der letzten Silbe betont wird.
>   *Beispiel:* begin – beginning
> - Ausnahme: *l* wird im British English auch dann verdoppelt, wenn die letzte Silbe nicht betont wird.
>   *Beispiel:* travel – travelling
>   Im American English schreibt man in diesem Fall nur ein *l*: traveling.

Aufgabe 10 Write the words correctly.

repeat + ing	_____	omit + ing	_____
differ + ed	_____	prefer + ed	_____
fulfil + ed	_____	permit + ed	_____
cancel + ed	_____		

6 Modale Hilfsverben

Im Gegensatz zu den Vollverben können Hilfsverben nicht alleine stehen. Sie sind immer mit einem Vollverb kombiniert. Die Hilfsverben *do, be* und *have* dienen u. a. dazu, die verschiedenen Zeitformen des Vollverbs zu bilden. Mit den **modalen Hilfsverben** *(modal auxiliaries)* können dagegen verschiedene **Sprechabsichten** ausgedrückt werden.

Du kannst modale Hilfsverben aufgrund der folgenden Punkte von Vollverben unterscheiden:

- Hilfsverben haben in der 3. Person Singular **kein -s**.
  Beispiele: He <u>must</u> go home now.
  Jane <u>cannot/can't</u> help you.

- **Fragen und Verneinungen** mit modalen Hilfsverben werden **ohne *to do*** gebildet.
  Beispiel: <u>Can</u> you help me?

- Modale Hilfsverben haben **keine Infinitiv- und keine Partizipform**.

- Modale Hilfsverben können nicht alle Zeitformen bilden. Manche Zeiten müssen deswegen mit **Ersatzformen** gebildet werden.
  Beispiele: He <u>must</u> go home.   *(present tense)*
  He <u>had to</u> go home.   *(past tense)*

6.1 *can / could*

Wie verwendest du die Formen von *can / could*?

can hat die Vergangenheitsform *could*. Das Futur und die zusammengesetzten Zeiten der Vergangenheit bildest du mit der Ersatzform *be able to*.
Beispiele: I <u>can</u> cook very well.
   I <u>will be able to</u> cook very well.

- *can* bzw. *can't* können eine **Fähigkeit** bzw. **Unfähigkeit**, eine **Erlaubnis** bzw. ein **Verbot**, eine **Möglichkeit** bzw. eine **Unmöglichkeit** ausdrücken.
  Beispiele: I <u>can</u> swim. I <u>can't</u> swim.   (Fähigkeit bzw. Unfähigkeit)
     You <u>can</u> have my bike. You <u>can't</u> have my bike.   (Erlaubnis bzw. Verbot)
     It <u>can</u> happen. It <u>can't</u> happen.   (Möglichkeit bzw. Unmöglichkeit)

- Fragen mit *can* und *could* drücken eine **Bitte** aus, dabei ist die Frage mit *could* höflicher.
  Beispiele: <u>Can</u> I have your bike?
     <u>Could</u> I have your bike?

Beachte: *could* bezeichnet in Kombination mit dem Infinitiv Perfekt eine mögliche Handlung in der Vergangenheit, die jedoch nicht ausgeführt wurde: *Why didn't you ask me? I could have helped you.* = Warum hast du mich nicht gefragt? Ich hätte dir helfen können.

... rund ums Verb: Modale Hilfsverben   69

Aufgabe 1   Birgit Schmid has received a letter from her English pen-friend, Sarah Lewis. Put these modal verbs in the correct tense into the gaps: *can, can't, able to, not able to.*

10, Abbey Road,
Billericay,
Essex CM12 9NF.
February 3rd, 2005

Dear Birgit,

Sorry I _____ to write to you till now but Greg and I have just got back from our cycling holiday in Tuscany. I _____ honestly say it was one of the best holidays I've ever had. Of course we _____ take much luggage with us, just a sleeping bag and a change of clothes! As you know you _____ put much in two pannier bags.

Although I _____ to ride a bike since I was six, most of my cycling has been to school or short cycling tours at weekends so I'm sure you can imagine how I felt after the first day of our holiday. In the evening we found a lovely little restaurant. The food was great, but the only problem was it was extremely painful to sit down and so I _____ really enjoy my meal!

As you know, Tuscany is very hilly! During the first week I _____ ride up the hills so I had to push my bike. Downhill of course was no problem. Anyway after a while I got a lot fitter and by the end of the two weeks I _____ to cycle up the steepest slopes.

As we _____ afford to stay in hotels we slept in the open air in our sleeping bags or quite often we _____ to find abandoned farm houses, where we _____ at least have a roof over our heads when the weather looked uncertain. One time we found a public wash house where the local women _____ wash and scrub their clothes. Most of them _____ do their washing at home because they haven't got washing machines. At 6 o'clock the following morning we were woken up by someone screaming at us: "You _____ sleep here, it's not a hotel. Get out or I'll call the police!" You _____ imagine how quickly we left!

I must say that was the only time during the whole holiday that someone was unfriendly to us. In the second week of our holiday I suddenly became ill. I had a high temperature and felt so bad that we _____ continue our tour. We _____ to find a bar on the main square of a little town called Chiustino where we _____ get help. The husband and wife who owned the bar were fantastic. They took me into their flat, called the doctor and told me that I _____ stay with them until I was better. Thanks to the way they looked after me, we _____ to continue our cycling holiday after three days.

Well, that's all my news for now. Have you been on holiday yet? I hope that you _____ to spend your summer holiday in England next year. Please give my regards to your parents and write soon!

Love,
Sarah

... rund ums Verb: Modale Hilfsverben

Aufgabe 2 Complete the short dialogues by putting *can, can't, able to* or *not able to* in the right tense:

a) ALAN: Dad, _____ I ask you something?
   DAD: Yes, of course you _____ .
   ALAN: Do you think I _____ borrow your car on Saturday?
   DAD: Your mother and I want to go to the theatre but we haven't bought the tickets yet. If we _____ get tickets, you _____ have it.

b) AMY: _____ you speak German?
   TOM: No, I'm afraid I _____ but I _____ speak a bit of French.

c) SUE: Have you seen the film "Titanic" yet?
   BOB: No I haven't. I wanted to go and see it on Friday but I _____ find a baby-sitter.
   SUE: I _____ baby-sit for you, if you like.

d) CARL: I've just seen an accident!
   TIM: Really, what happened?
   CARL: Well, a car knocked over a cyclist and just drove away!
   TIM: _____ (you) write down the number of the licence plate?
   CARL: I _____ write it down if I'd had a piece of paper and a pen but unfortunately I didn't have my bag with me.

e) NIK: Take an umbrella with you. It _____ rain.
   LIZ: No, I never take umbrellas with me. I've lost so many umbrellas! I _____ never remember where I leave them!

f) JIM: I wish I _____ ski as well as you _____ !
   ABBY: It's only because I've had a lot more practice. I was born near the Alps and I _____ ski since I was three. Most of the children in the village where I come from _____ ski before they _____ walk.

g) JOE: I _____ do this translation. _____ you help me?
   SANDY: Sorry, I haven't got time now. If you'd asked me yesterday I _____ helped you.

6.2 may / might

Wie gebrauchst du die Formen von *may / might*?

may wird für das Präsens und das Futur verwendet, die anderen Zeiten werden mit den Ersatzformen *be possible* and *be allowed to* gebildet. Die Kurzform *mayn't (may + not)* ist veraltet, *mightn't (might + not)* ist dagegen gebräuchlich.

- *may* kann eine **Möglichkeit** oder eine **Erlaubnis** bzw. ein **Verbot** ausdrücken. Bitten mit *may* sind förmlicher als Bitten mit *can*.

  Beispiele: You <u>may</u> be right. (Möglichkeit)
  You <u>may</u> park here. You <u>may</u> <u>not</u> smoke here. (Erlaubnis bzw. Verbot)
  <u>May</u> I use your phone? (Bitte um Erlaubnis)

- *might* drückt eine **Möglichkeit** oder eine **Bitte um Erlaubnis** aus. *might* wird in Bitten verwendet, wenn sich der Fragende unsicher ist, ob seine Bitte erfüllt wird. *can/could* in einer Frage bedeutet, dass der Fragende sicher ist, dass seine Bitte erfüllt wird.

  Beispiele: He <u>might</u> be still asleep. (Möglichkeit)
  "<u>Might</u> I borrow your car for tonight?" (Bitte um Erlaubnis)

- *may / might* + **Infinitiv Perfekt** drücken eine **Annahme** über Handlungen in der Vergangenheit aus.

  Beispiel: John <u>may/might</u> have arrived. (Vermutlich ist John schon angekommen.)

Aufgabe 3 What would you say in these situations? Use *may, may not, might* or *might not*.

a) Du erzählst einer Freundin, wo du vielleicht deinen nächsten Urlaub verbringst. Möglicherweise fährst du nach Irland.

b) Du fragst die Mutter deines Freundes ob du telefonieren darfst.

c) Du bist im Urlaub bei deinem englischen Brieffreund. Frag ihn, ob du sein nagelneues Mountainbike probieren darfst.

d) Sag deiner Freundin, sie soll vorsichtig sein, weil der Weg eisig sein könnte.

e) Jemand fragt dich, ob du Tony zu deinem Geburtstagsfest eingeladen hast. Antworte, dass du ihn nicht eingeladen hast, aber du hättest ihn vielleicht eingeladen, wenn du ihn besser gekannt hättest.

f) Sag deiner Mutter, dass du eventuell später von der Schule heim kommst, weil du mit einer Freundin in die Stadt gehen willst.

g) Deine Mutter ist nicht zu Hause, wenn du von der Schule nach Hause kommst. Sag deinem Bruder, dass du vermutest, dass sie einkaufen gegangen ist.

h) Bitte deinen Freund heute Abend, nicht anzurufen, weil du möglicherweise englische Vokabeln lernst, da du morgen eventuell einen Test schreibst.

6.3 will / would

Wie verwendest du *will / would*?

will hat in weniger formellen Texten die Kurzform *'ll* sowie die verneinte Kurzform *won't*.
would hat die Kurzform *'d* sowie die verneinte Kurzform *wouldn't*.
Beachte: *He'd come* kann sowohl *he would come* (er würde kommen), als auch *he had come* (er war gekommen) ausdrücken. Die jeweilige Zeit ergibt sich aus dem Textzusammenhang.

- *will* und *would* können als modale Hilfsverben eine **Bitte**, ein **Angebot** bzw. eine **Einladung**, eine **Wahrscheinlichkeit** oder ein **typisches Verhalten** ausdrücken. Die Frage mit *would* ist höflicher als die Frage mit *will* und wird deshalb häufiger verwendet.

  Beispiele: Will / would you please pass me the salt?   (Bitte)
  Will you have another cup of tea?   (Angebot, Einladung)
  He will be in London by now.   (Wahrscheinlichkeit)
  He would have been ill at that time.
  On holiday Jane will read for hours.   (typisches Verhalten)
  At the weekends the boys would go to Wembley stadium.
  (Im Deutschen wird dieses *would* mit ‚pflegten' wiedergegeben.)

> - In der verneinten Form können *won't* und *wouldn't* eine **Weigerung** ausdrücken. *wouldn't* wird dabei zum Ausdruck einer Weigerung in der Vergangenheit verwendet.
>   Beispiele: Tom won't admit that he made a mistake.
>   The doctor told him to stop smoking, but Ben wouldn't.
> - *will* kann auch zum Ausdruck eines **Befehls** verwendet werden.
>   Beispiel: You will do as I told you.

Aufgabe 4 What would you say in the following situations? Use *will* or *would*.

a) Du bist in einem Restaurant und möchtest bezahlen. Frage den Ober, ob er dir die Rechnung bringen kann.

b) Biete deiner Freundin noch ein Stück Kuchen an.

c) Frage deinen Freund, ob er heute Abend mit dir ins Kino gehen möchte.

d) Sage deinem Freund, dass er zuhören soll.

e) Sage deinem Lehrer, dass es dir leid tut, zu spät dran zu sein, aber dein Auto ist nicht angesprungen.

f) Erzähle einer Freundin, dass dir dein Vater jeden Abend eine Geschichte vorzulesen pflegte.

g) Bitte deine Mutter, dir bei deiner Hausaufgabe zu helfen.

h) Deine Mutter hat starke Kopfschmerzen. Biete ihr an, ihr ein Aspirin zu bringen. Sage ihr, dass sie sich bald besser fühlen wird.

i) Sage deinem Bruder, dass er die Wohnzimmertür schließen soll.

j) Du hast den Bus verpasst. Frage deine Mutter, ob sie dich zur Schule fährt.

6.4 shall / should

> **Wie verwendest du *shall / should*?**
>
> *shall* hat wie *will* die Kurzformen *I'll*, *you'll* usw. Die verneinte Kurzform lautet *shan't*.
> *should* hat wie *would* die Kurzformen *I'd*, *you'd* usw. *You'd come* kann sowohl ‚du würdest kommen' als auch ‚du solltest kommen' heißen. Die jeweilige Bedeutung ergibt sich aus dem Textzusammenhang. Die verneinte Kurzform lautet *shouldn't*.
>
> - *shall* kann ein **Angebot**, einen **Vorschlag** und eine **Bitte um Anweisung** ausdrücken:
>   Beispiele: <u>Shall</u> I help you? (Angebot)
>   <u>Shall</u> we go to a Chinese restaurant? (Vorschlag)
>   Where <u>shall</u> I put the key? (Bitte um Anweisung)
>
> - *should* kann einen **Ratschlag** und eine **Verpflichtung** ausdrücken. *should* + Infinitiv Perfekt drückt eine **Verpflichtung in der Vergangenheit** aus, die nicht erfüllt wurde. *should* + *not* + Infinitiv Perfekt bedeutet, dass **eine Handlung in der Vergangenheit nicht hätte ausgeführt werden** sollen. Zum Ausdruck eines Ratschlages oder einer Verpflichtung kannst du auch *ought to* verwenden.
>   Beispiele: You <u>should</u> put on your boots. (Ratschlag)
>   You <u>should</u> keep within the speed limit. (Verpflichtung)
>   You <u>should</u> have switched on the headlights.
>   (unerfüllte Verpflichtung in der Vergangenheit)
>   You <u>shouldn't</u> have braked suddenly.
>   (Handlung, die nicht hätte ausgeführt werden sollen)
>   You <u>ought not/oughtn't</u> to overtake this car, it's going very fast.

Aufgabe 5 Write new sentences using *shall* or *should*.

a) It would have been good if you had come to the party. It was great.

_____

b) You look tired. I advise you to go to bed.

_____

c) I feel sick. It would have been better if I hadn't eaten so much.

_____

d) It would be better not to allow smoking in restaurants.

_____

e) I think Margaret has got a good chance of passing her driving test.

_____

f) Would you like me to carry your bags? They look very heavy.

_____

g) I suggest having a game of tennis on Saturday.

h) What do you suggest I buy: the blue jeans or the black ones?

i) These chocolate biscuits are delicious. Why don't you try one?

j) If I were you, I would have my hair cut before your interview.

k) Would you like me to gift-wrap it?

6.5 *must / mustn't / needn't*

Wie verwendest du *must / mustn't*?

must tritt nur im Präsens auf. Alle anderen Zeiten werden mit der Ersatzform *have (got) to* gebildet. Die entsprechenden Zeiten von *mustn't* werden mit *not to be allowed to* gebildet. *needn't* tritt meist nur im Präsens auf und wird in den übrigen Zeitformen durch *not to have to* ersetzt.

- *must* kann einen **Zwang** oder eine **Schlussfolgerung** ausdrücken. Zum Ausdruck eines Zwanges kannst du neben *must* auch *have (got) to* verwenden. *must* drückt dabei häufig einen Zwang aus, den **der Sprecher auferlegt**, während *have (got) to* einen Zwang ausdrückt, **der durch äußere Umstände bedingt ist**.
  Beispiele: Today you must work overtime. (Zwang)
  Be careful, it has rained. The roads must be wet. (Schlussfolgerung)
  You must leave at six. (vom Sprecher ausgeübter Zwang)
  You have (got) to change at Birmingham. (durch äußere Umstände bedingter Zwang)

- *mustn't* wird verwendet, um ein **Verbot** auszudrücken. Neben *mustn't* drückt auch *be not to* ein Verbot aus. Während bei *mustn't* das Verbot meistens vom Sprecher ausgeht, verwendest du *be not to* bei Verboten, die von anderen Instanzen ausgesprochen wurden.
  Beispiele: You mustn't disturb me now. (Verbot des Sprechers)
  You are not to disturb the manager now. (andere Instanz)

- *needn't* drückt das **Fehlen eines Zwanges** aus.
  Beispiel: You needn't take a taxi, there is an hourly bus service to the town centre.

76 ... rund ums Verb: Modale Hilfsverben

Aufgabe 6 Put in *must, mustn't, have to* or *needn't* into the gaps in the following advertisement.

Join the Police!

A career in the Police Force is something any young person looking for a job with adventure and responsibility _____ consider. If you decide to join us, you _____ worry about having the necessary self-confidence.

We'll train you and help you develop the self-confidence to cope in even the trickiest situation.

A job with the Police is sometimes complicated but never boring! Flexibility and quick thinking are very important because you may find yourself in situations where a quick decision could save lives!

In the Police you _____ sometimes deal with drunks, investigate burglaries or from time to time you might just _____ help an old lady who has locked herself out. We need young people who are prepared to take on responsibility, are decisive and of course you _____ be fit. However if you're not fit when you join us you certainly will be after the preliminary ten-week training period! In some situations you _____ keep calm and _____ panic. This is something else you will learn in the first ten weeks at Training School, before going out on the streets with an experienced Officer to help you and advise you.

If you join us you _____ spend half of your salary on somewhere to live because we offer generous rent allowances or even free accommodation!

One more thing which _____ be left out is that we offer equal career chances for men and women.

Applicants _____ be under 18. Men _____ be at least 172 cms tall and women _____ be over 161 cms tall.

If you'd like to know more, send for our brochure now.

... rund ums Verb: Modale Hilfsverben 77

Aufgabe 7* Mixed exercise: Choose a suitable modal verb in the right tense for each of the gaps in the following texts.

Here are some jokes about restaurants:

a) Mr Smith finished his breakfast. Then he asked the waiter if he _____ fetch the manager of the hotel.
"Yes, sir, what _____ I do for you?" said the hotel manager when he arrived at Mr Smith's table.
"You _____ have a very clean kitchen here," said Mr Smith.
"I _____ say that's very kind of you to say so, sir, but _____ I ask why you think our kitchen is so clean?"
"Well", replied Mr Smith, "Everything tastes of soap!"

b) A foreign visitor to England _____ eat the food his landlady served him. At last he _____ say something to her about it.
"I don't like this pie, Mrs Perkins," he said.
"Oh, _____ you tell me what's wrong with it?" said Mrs Perkins angrily. "I was making pies before you were born."
"This _____ be one of them!" replied Mr Schmidt.

c) Mr Clarke was staying in a small hotel by the sea. It wasn't a good hotel and the meals were extremely small. All the visitors _____ have their meals at the same time. Mr Clarke got the last plate. It looked wet. He held it up to the waitress and said: "You _____ dried this plate properly. It looks wet. _____ you bring me another one please."
"That's your soup", replied the waitress.

Aufgabe 8* Mixed exercise – Prince William of Wales: Put in a suitable modal auxiliary with the verb in brackets in the right tense into the gaps in the following text.

Some people think that Queen Elizabeth II. _____ (give up) the throne years ago so that her son and heir, Prince Charles _____ (take over). However others say that Prince William, Charles' oldest son _____ (become) king instead of his father.
William, the attractive, blonde Prince, already the heart-throb of so many teenage girls, is rather shy and probably sometimes _____ (like) to be a completely ordinary young man who _____ (walk) down the street without anybody recognising him.

The Prince _____ (go) anywhere alone. They _____ (be) accompanied at all times by at least one bodyguard. They have almost no private life because they _____ (take part) in many official occasions. They _____ (go) to parties or have a date with a girl without the whole world knowing about and the older they get, the worse it will be.
One _____ (hope) that after the death of their mother, Princess Diana, who _____ (do) anything without being hounded by reporters and photographers, the press will have pity on William and Harry and leave them in peace.
Prince Harry is less popular in the eye of the public than his brother William. One reason _____ (be) that he does not resemble his mother, "The Queen of Hearts" like his brother. He wants to become an officer in the Armed Forces. He will _____ (enroll) at the Military Academy of Sandhurst. To be admitted, he _____ (be) in good physical condition. The Academy also expects moral qualities.
As William and Harry are not always on their best behaviour, their father has decided that they _____ (have) advisers to help them how to act in public. These advisers have repeatedly been criticized. Some people demand that Prince Charles _____ (find) better ones.
One thing is certain, with William's looks and character he _____ (be) a very popular King. He _____ (be) more popular than his grandmother, Queen Elizabeth II.

... rund ums Verb: Modale Hilfsverben / 79

> **Zusammensetzungen** *(compounds)*
> Auch mit Partizipien, die auf *-ing* enden *(present participles)*, kann man Zusammensetzungen bilden. Sie werden meist mit Bindestrich geschrieben.
> *Beispiel:* an occupation which consumes a lot of time = a <u>time-consuming</u> occupation

Aufgabe 9 Find the correct *-ing* form.

eine Aussicht, die einem den Atem (breath) nimmt   a _____ view

etwas, das eine weit reichende Wirkung hat   a _____ effect

ein Popstar, der gut aussieht   a _____ popstar

ein lässiges Leben; ein Leben, das man leicht nimmt   a _____ life

> **Wörter mit einem stummen -e am Ende**
> - Das stumme *-e* entfällt, wenn eine Endung, die mit einem Vokal beginnt, angehängt wird.
>   *Beispiel:* love: loving, lovable
>   aber: lovely
>   Ausnahmen: see + ing = seeing, agree + ing = agreeing, agree + able = agreeable
> - Wörter, die auf *-ce* und *-ge* enden, behalten das stumme *-e*, wenn eine Endung angehängt wird, die nicht mit *-e* oder *-i* beginnt.
>   *Beispiel:* change + ing = changing
>   aber: change + able = changeable

Aufgabe 10 Write the words correctly.

name + ed	_____	name + less	_____
praise + worthy	_____	praise + ing	_____
hope + ful	_____	believe + able	_____
replace + ing	_____	courage + ous	_____
noise + less	_____	prace + ious	_____

7 Gerundium

Das Gerundium *(gerund)* ist eine **infinite Form** des Verbs. „Infinit" bedeutet, dass diese Form nichts über Person und Zeit aussagt. Infinite Formen wie das Gerundium, das Partizip Präsens und der Infinitiv sind typische Verbformen des Englischen, die häufig verwendet werden und bei der Übersetzung ins Deutsche oft mit anderen Konstruktionen wiedergegeben werden müssen.

Wie bildest du das Gerundium?

Ein Gerundium kann von jedem Vollverb durch Anfügen der **Endung -ing** gebildet werden. Es hat somit die gleiche Form wie das Partizip Präsens, von dem es sich jedoch durch seine Funktion im Satz unterscheidet.

Beispiele: Walking is healthy. (Gerundium)
There's my brother walking towards the house. (Partizip)

Wann verwendest du das Gerundium?

Da das Gerundium eine Form ist, die sowohl Elemente des Verbs als auch Elemente des Nomens aufweist, kann es im Satz verschiedene Funktionen übernehmen:

1. Das Gerundium als Subjekt
Beispiel: Swimming is a nice hobby.

2. Das Gerundium als Ergänzung nach Präpositionen
- Substantiv + Präposition + Gerundium

the opportunity of	die Gelegenheit …
the advantage of	der Vorteil …
the chance of	die Chance …
the danger of	die Gefahr …
the hope of	die Hoffnung …
the way of	die Art …
the possibility of	die Möglichkeit …
the dislike of	die Abneigung …
the difficulty in	die Schwierigkeit …
the problem in	das Problem …
the interest in	das Interesse …
the reason for	der Grund …
the place for + Gerundium	der Ort …

- Verb + Präposition + Gerundium

to accuse of	anklagen wegen
to dream of	träumen von
to think of	denken an
to consist of	bestehen aus
to die of	sterben an
to begin by	beginnen mit
to cope with	fertig werden mit
to succeed in	erfolgreich sein mit
to specialize in	sich spezialisieren auf
to take part in	teilnehmen an
to rely on	sich verlassen auf
to concentrate on	sich konzentrieren auf
to depend on	abhängen von
to prevent from	hindern an
to escape from	fliehen vor
to apologise for	sich entschuldigen für

- Adjektiv + Präposition + Gerundium

afraid of	etwas befürchten
tired of	genug haben von
fond of	sehr gerne mögen
ashamed of	sich schämen wegen
clever at	gut in
disappointed at	enttäuscht über
surprised at	überrascht über
crazy about	verrückt nach
delighted about	sehr erfreut über
enthusiastic about	begeistert über
excited about	aufgeregt über
glad about	froh über
famous for	berühmt wegen
necessary for	notwendig für
useful for	nützlich für
keen on	begeistert von
accustomed to	gewöhnt an
impressed with	beeindruckt von

Aufgabe 1 Walt Disney: Complete the sentences with the missing preposition and the correct form of the verb.

a) As a child Walt Disney lived on his parents' farm where he had the chance _____ (watch) animal behaviour.

... rund ums Verb: Gerundium

b) At school his teachers gave him the opportunity _____ (draw) and (act) _____.

c) The reason _____ (move) to a town was his father's interest _____ (write) articles for newspapers.

d) Walt had a dislike _____ (deliver) newspapers as a newspaper boy.

e) During World War I, Walt was often in danger _____ (be killed) in his job as an ambulance driver.

f) When he returned after the war, he found a place _____ (start) a film company in Kansas.

g) When his company failed, he moved to California in the hope _____ (found) a new company together with his brother, Roy.

h) In 1928 Walt Disney made history _____ (create) Mickey Mouse.

i) With Mickey Mouse, Disney had the advantage _____ (earn) a lot of money with which he could pay artists to work for him.

j) The success of animated cartoons gave Walt Disney the chance _____ (work) on the first animated film, "Snow White and the Seven Dwarfs".

Aufgabe 2 Mickey Mouse: Complete the sentences with the missing preposition and the correct form of the verb.

a) Walt Disney concentrated _____ (make) animated films.

b) Mickey Mouse succeeded _____ (become) Disney's most popular cartoon character.

c) Walt Disney spent much time and money _____ (invent) Donald Duck and Goofy who were even more successful than Mickey Mouse in the 40s.

d) At first the artists' work in shaping Mickey Mouse consisted _____ (draw) circles for head, body and ears. In later years the artists coped _____ (make) Mickey more expressive.

e) Later changes consisted _____ (give) Mickey new, more modern costumes and bigger eyes.

f) Walt Disney relied _____ (have) a good team of artists and composers.

g) From 1928 to 1995 Walt Disney specialised _____ (make) Mickey Mouse films, 120 altogether.

h) Walt Disney always dreamt _____ (build) a new Disneyland in Europe. It was realized in 1992 near Paris.

i) Many parents were angry with their children for sitting in front of the TV all day long, but they could not prevent them _____ (watch) Mickey's adventures.

j) Walt Disney always thought _____ (take) chances on the animated films market.

Aufgabe 3   Disneyland: Complete the sentences with the missing preposition and the correct form of the verb.

a) Walt Disney was proud _____ (open) the first fun park in Anaheim, California, in 1955.

b) From the start children and parents have been enthusiastic _____ (visit) the park.

c) His designers were clever _____ (build) attractive sights like castles or Western towns.

d) Children are crazy _____ (go) on trains, steamers and merry-go-rounds.

e) Guests are delighted _____ (watch) wild animals in the park.

f) The kids are never tired _____ (watch) parades and celebrations.

g) Tourist officials throughout the world are keen _____ (build) parks like Disneyland.

h) The Disney Company's permission is necessary _____ (imitate) Disneyland parks.

84 ... rund ums Verb: Gerundium

i) Disneyland near Paris is famous _____ (have) old, romantic castles.

j) Visitors to the Disney Park in Anaheim are most surprised _____ (be able) to go on a real jungle cruise and _____ (be allowed) to have a ride on a fire-engine.

Aufgabe 4 What George Orwell's "Animal Farm" is about: Join the two sentences using a prepositional phrase and a gerund.

a) What does George Orwell aim at in his novel? – He shows that revolutions are always followed by tyranny.

_____

_____

b) The farmer, Mr Jones, treats the animals badly. – He is accustomed to this treatment.

_____

_____

c) The animals dream of their freedom. – They want to be free.

_____

d) They want to drive out their human master, Mr Jones. – They are very keen on it.

_____

e) Mr Jones escapes. – He runs away.

_____

f) The animals choose two boars, Napoleon and Snowball, as their leaders. – The animals all agree with the election.

_____

g) Napoleon and Snowball are clever. – They are proud of their cleverness.

_____

h) For some time the animals live in peace. – They are glad about it.

i) But Napoleon wants to be the master of the farm. – He is interested in this position.

j) The dogs forming Napoleon's bodyguard help him. – They drive Snowball away.

k) The pigs try to be like their former master. – They begin to walk on their hind legs.

l) Napoleon tries to form an alliance with nearby human farmers. – He succeeds in it.

m) The animals dare not protest. – They are afraid of this.

n) The animals cannot live in freedom. – Napoleon prevents them from it.

o) He oppresses the animals just as their former master, Mr Jones, oppressed them. – He says: "All animals are equal, but some are more equal than others."

3. Das Gerundium als Objekt

Das Gerundium steht in Verbindung mit einigen **Verben**. Die häufigsten Verben, die ein Gerundium fordern, sind:

to admit	zugeben
to appreciate	zu schätzen wissen
to avoid	vermeiden
to consider	betrachten, halten für, denken an

to delay	verschieben, aufschieben
to deny	bestreiten, ableugnen
to detest	verabscheuen, hassen
to enjoy	genießen, gerne etwas tun
to escape	flüchten, entfliehen
to finish	beenden, aufhören
to hate	hassen, jemanden nicht ausstehen können
can't help	nichts dafür können
to keep	behalten, etwas weiter tun
to mention	erwähnen
to mind	aufpassen, achten auf
to miss	versäumen, nicht bekommen oder schaffen
to object to	dagegen sein, Einwände haben
to practise	üben, ausüben
to risk	riskieren
can't stand	nicht aushalten

4. Das Gerundium nach festen Wendungen

it's fun	es macht Spaß
it's no good	es hat keinen Sinn
it's hard	es ist schwierig
it's a pleasure	es ist ein Vergnügen
it's no use	es hat keinen Sinn
it's useless	es ist sinnlos

Aufgabe 5 Emigrating: Complete the sentences.

John and Helen Robertson from Glasgow (hatten lange erwogen – emigrate) _____ to Australia _____. John (konnte nicht mehr ertragen – work) _____ in a noisy ship-yard _____. Helen wanted to (aufhören – type) _____ letters as a secretary day after day. One evening Helen (schlug vor – go) _____ to Australia. From that day onwards the Robertsons (konnten nicht umhin – discuss) _____ the matter again and again. In 1997 they could not (aufschieben – make) _____ a decision any longer: "We are leaving Britain for Australia." In April 1998 John left first. He knew he did not (riskieren – be) _____ unemployed – there were more jobs than in Britain. Helen did not (aufschieben – follow) _____ him; she left Britain three months later. John (schlug vor – settle down) _____ in Sydney. Helen (gibt zu – feel) _____ homesick at first. Both (schätzen es – live) _____ in one of the world's most fascinating capitals. They don't (haben nichts dagegen – have) _____ longer working hours than in Britain. They found a flat

near the sea and they (haben viel Spaß – swim and surf) _____.
John (gibt zu – go) _____ to another country to live and work there is a huge risk. Helen does not (leugnen – have) _____ problems with the life in a new country. She says: "Sometimes it's like being in paradise, but there are also times which are very hard."

Aufgabe 6   Questionnaire: Complete the questions.

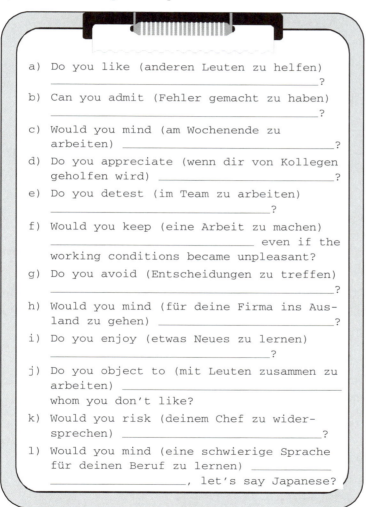

a) Do you like (anderen Leuten zu helfen) _____?
b) Can you admit (Fehler gemacht zu haben) _____?
c) Would you mind (am Wochenende zu arbeiten) _____?
d) Do you appreciate (wenn dir von Kollegen geholfen wird) _____?
e) Do you detest (im Team zu arbeiten) _____?
f) Would you keep (eine Arbeit zu machen) _____ even if the working conditions became unpleasant?
g) Do you avoid (Entscheidungen zu treffen) _____?
h) Would you mind (für deine Firma ins Ausland zu gehen) _____?
i) Do you enjoy (etwas Neues zu lernen) _____?
j) Do you object to (mit Leuten zusammen zu arbeiten) _____ whom you don't like?
k) Would you risk (deinem Chef zu widersprechen) _____?
l) Would you mind (eine schwierige Sprache für deinen Beruf zu lernen) _____, let's say Japanese?

Aufgabe 7 Jobs: Complete the sentences with the correct expressions.
a) Nowadays _____ finding a job after one's own heart.
b) _____ applying for a job in a travel agency, if you don't speak one or two foreign languages.
c) _____ learning Spanish, because of the South American Continent.
d) _____ being a surfing instructor in the Bahamas as a holiday job.
e) I doubt whether it is always _____ animating people in a holiday club.
f) There's _____ that being able to use a computer is an indispensable qualification when applying for a job.
g) _____ arriving early for a job interview.
h) _____ exaggerating one's abilities when talking to a job interviewer.

Aufgabe 8 Mixed exercise: Walt Disney's world hits – The Jungle Book.
Tell the story in English.
a) Mowgli, a human boy (ist daran gewöhnt, mit Wölfen im indischen Dschungel zu leben) _____.
b) As Shere Khan, the tiger, wants to kill him, his friends (denken daran, ihn in die Zivilisation zurückzuschicken) _____.
c) Mowgli (ist darüber verärgert, dass er seine Freunde verlassen muss) _____.
d) (Es hat keinen Sinn zu bleiben) _____ because Shere Khan has vowed to kill him.
e) Bagheera the panther (hat viele Schwierigkeiten, ihn zu begleiten) _____ because Mowgli is unwilling to leave the jungle.
f) With the help of his friends, Bagheera and Baloo the bear, (gelingt es Mowgli, den Tiger zu besiegen) _____.

g) Soon after (Mowgli ist entzückt darüber, Kitty, die Tochter eines englischen Majors zu treffen) _____.

h) Now (er hat nichts dagegen, in die Zivilisation zurückzukehren) _____.

i) As the artists of the animated film (sie hatten Schwierigkeiten, die Bewegungen der vielen verschiedenen Tiere zu imitieren) _____ the film company built a little zoo with tigers, leopards, wolves, bears, elephants and monkeys – all in all 52 animals – where they could study the way these animals move.

j) The film (ist es wert, gesehen zu werden) _____ also because of its Oscar nominated songs "I wanna be like you", "That's what friends are for" and Baloo's famous "Bare necessities".

8 Infinitiv

Der Infinitiv *(infinitive)* ist die Grundform des Verbs. Er kann mit oder ohne *to* stehen und hat sowohl Aktiv- als auch Passivformen.

Beispiele:	Peter wants <u>to go</u> to the cinema.	(Aktiv, mit *to*)
	The rules ought <u>to be obeyed</u>.	(Passiv, mit *to*)
	Peter might <u>go</u> to the cinema tomorrow.	(Aktiv, ohne *to*)
	The rules must <u>be obeyed</u>.	(Passiv, ohne *to*)

8.1 Verwendung des Infinitivs

Wann verwendest du den Infinitiv ohne *to*?

- Der Infinitiv ohne *to* steht nach ***make* + Objekt** mit der Bedeutung ‚veranlassen, anordnen', nach ***let* + Objekt** mit der Bedeutung ‚zulassen, erlauben' und nach ***let's***, um einen Vorschlag auszudrücken.

    Beispiele: The manager <u>made</u> the workers <u>work</u> overtime.
    The manager <u>let</u> the secretary <u>go</u> home earlier than usual because she felt ill.
    Let's <u>have</u> a drink.

- Der Infinitiv ohne *to* steht nach allen **Hilfsverben**, ausgenommen *ought to*.

    Beispiel: You <u>must</u>/<u>can't</u>/<u>may</u>/<u>should</u> leave now.

- Der Infinitiv ohne *to* **nach festen Wendungen:** Der Infinitiv ohne *to* steht nach *why not*, wobei diese Wendung einen Vorschlag ausdrückt. Außerdem steht der Infinitiv ohne *to* nach *had better/had better not* zum Ausdruck eines Ratschlages. Der Infinitiv ohne *to* nach *would rather/would rather not* drückt eine Vorliebe oder Abneigung aus.

    Beispiele: <u>Why not take</u> a taxi?
    You <u>had better</u> put on a warm coat.
    I <u>would rather</u> stay at home.

- Der Infinitiv ohne *to* **nach Verben der Sinneswahrnehmung** *(see, hear, watch, notice* usw.): Der Infinitiv ohne *to* steht nach Verben der Sinneswahrnehmung, wenn mehrere Handlungen aufeinander folgen. Außerdem steht der Infinitiv ohne *to*, wenn betont wird, dass eine Handlung beendet wurde.

    Beispiele: The witness said that she had <u>seen</u> the car <u>come</u> nearer, <u>stop</u> and <u>start</u> again.
    I <u>saw</u> the man <u>swim</u> across the river.
    (Die Betonung liegt auf *schwimmen*, nicht *rudern* oder Ähnliches.)

... rund ums Verb: Infinitiv

Aufgabe 1 New atomic terror: Fill in *make/made/making* or *let/let's*.

a) In May 1998, New Delhi's government _____ atomic bombs explode in a desert near the borders of its neighbour Pakistan.

b) The world is shaken, it does not want to _____ India's nuclear power grow.

c) It is not in the nation's interest to _____ its security become weaker.

d) India tried to _____ the world believe that its nuclear tests were harmless.

e) US spy satellites _____ the White House know about the nuclear tests.

f) The United Nations do not want to _____ India continue its nuclear tests.

g) The President of Russia, Boris Yeltsin, appealed to the 149 nations that signed the test-ban treaty: "_____ do our utmost to settle this new nuclear problem."

Aufgabe 2 Agatha Christie: Fill in *make* or *let*.

Dame Agatha Mary Clarissa Christie, Britain's most famous detective novelist was born in 1890 in Torquay, Cornwall.
Her mother did not _____ her go to school, because she thought that no child should read until the age of eight. Agatha's father had made a lot of money in the US, and this money _____ the family live at ease. However, Agatha was keen on reading and she _____ her mother teach her how to read.
When she was eleven, the local newspaper _____ her publish a poem she had written: "When the first electric tram did run." As Agatha liked music, her parents _____ her study music in Paris at the age of sixteen, but she wasn't good enough and her teachers _____ her give up her hopes of a concert career. A few years later, she started her career as a writer of detective stories telling the adventures of "Hercule Poirot" and "Miss Marple".
Back in Torquay she was engaged to a gentleman, but she fell in love with a young officer, Archibald Christie. She _____ her fiancé know that she wanted to break off the engagement and married a man, she had only known for a few days.

If you want to read one (or more) of Agatha Christie's detective stories, here is a choice for you:

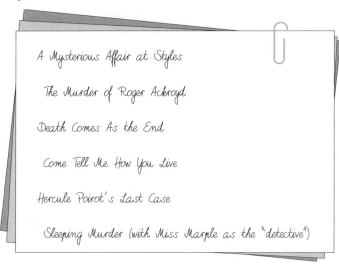

A Mysterious Affair at Styles

The Murder of Roger Ackroyd

Death Comes As the End

Come Tell Me How You Live

Hercule Poirot's Last Case

Sleeping Murder (with Miss Marple as the "detective")

Aufgabe 3 Fill in the appropriate expression.

TOM: _____ go to Peter's party tonight?
BILL: I _____, Peter's such a bore.
JOAN: You _____ accept his invitation, Bill. After all Peter's a good friend of ours.
TOM: Joan is right. You _____ stay at home this evening.
BILL: There's a good film on TV tonight, Miss Marple, with Margaret Rutherford. I _____ see it and come later.

Aufgabe 4 The burglary: Complete the sentences with the infinitive or the present participle of the given verbs: *search, climb, arrive, ring up, escape, go, open, say*.

a) In the middle of the night, the Parkers woke up. They heard someone _____ into the house through an open window, _____ into the living room and _____ the cupboard.

b) Mrs Parker heard her husband _____ (abgeschlossene Handlung) the police.

c) Mr Parker hurried downstairs and saw a man _____ (Handlung soll betont werden) through the window.
d) A few minutes later, the Parkers heard the police car _____ (abgeschlossene Handlung).
e) The Parkers watched the policemen _____ (Handlung soll betont werden) for fingerprints. They did not find any.
f) The burglar had stolen the Parkers' silver cutlery. Mrs Parker heard one of the policemen _____ (abgeschlossene Handlung), "This is a case for Miss Marple."

Wann verwendest du den Infinitiv mit *to*?

- Der Infinitiv mit *to* nach **Verben**: Der Infinitiv mit *to* steht nach Verben, die eine **Absicht** oder einen **Wunsch** ausdrücken (z. B. *hope, intend, wish, expect, would like*) und nach Verben, die einen **Rat**, eine **Aufforderung** oder eine **Erlaubnis** ausdrücken (z. B. *advise, recommend, ask, beg, persuade, encourage, command, force, allow, permit*).
  Beispiele: I plan to leave tomorrow.
  I want to find a job in the movie business.
  He advised me to take a taxi.
  He encouraged me to take up this job.
  The manager allowed us to enter.

- Der Infinitiv mit *to* nach **Adjektiven**: Der Infinitiv mit *to* steht nach Adjektiven, die ein **Gefühl** ausdrücken.
  Beispiel: I was surprised to hear that he was on holiday.

- Der Infinitiv mit *to* steht nach *it + be + Adjektiv*. Mit diesen Verbindungen können die **Schwierigkeit**, etwas zu tun, eine **gefühlsmäßige Wirkung** oder **Lob und Kritik** ausgedrückt werden.
  Beispiele: It is difficult to do my homework.
  It is pleasant to go walking in the sunshine.
  It is right to go to bed early if you are tired.

- Der Infinitiv mit *to* steht nach **Adjektiven**, die eine **Wahrscheinlichkeit** ausdrücken. Im Deutschen verwendet man dafür eine andere (adverbielle) Struktur.
  Beispiel: John is likely to come. (= John kommt wahrscheinlich.)

94 ... rund ums Verb: Infinitiv

Aufgabe 5 Holiday plans: Tell your friend about your plans for the holidays.

Du planst, nach England zu fahren.
Du möchtest gerne Stonehenge besichtigen.
Du wünschst dir, Prinz Charles zu begegnen.
Du beabsichtigst, in Wales ein Pony zu mieten.
Du erwartest, dass die Sonne die ganze Zeit scheint.
Du hoffst, dort neue Freunde zu finden.
Du ziehst es vor, in deinem Zelt zu übernachten.

Aufgabe 6 The flight to London: Complete the sentences by translating the words in brackets.

As most airlines allow 20 kg of luggage, my mother (riet mir, ich solle prüfen) _____ the weight of my suitcase at home. She (empfahl mir, ich solle nicht tragen) _____ anyone else's luggage through the customs. At the check-in counter the ground hostess (sagte mir, ich solle befestigen) _____ my luggage label to my suitcase. A friend of mine (bat mich, ich solle fotografieren) _____ of the Channel from above, if there were no clouds. On the plane I had a seat in the middle of a row. When we were flying over Brussels, the lady next to me (erlaubte mir zu tauschen) _____ my seat for her window-seat. Before we landed at Heathrow, the pilot (forderte uns auf anzulegen) _____ our seat belts. At the customs, the officer (zwang zu öffnen) _____ one of the passengers _____ his suitcase. As I had nothing to declare (wurde mir erlaubt zu verlassen) _____ the arrival hall without any problems.

Aufgabe 7 How people feel about ... (something): Rewrite the sentences using an infinitive.

a) I should be delighted if I could help you.

b) I'm glad now that I see you are no longer depressed.

c) They will be very surprised when they hear this news.

d) We were shocked when we heard of the accident.

e) Vivian was worried when she saw that her boyfriend was ill.

f) Of course Peter was very pleased when he found a new job.

g) Kevin's parents were sad when they heard that he had failed his exam.

h) We were sorry when we saw that a car had injured the dog.

i) Carol was happy when she found out that she hadn't lost her car key.

j) I'm sorry but I must tell you that you didn't win the race.

Aufgabe 8 What people think of … (something): Rewrite the sentences using an infinitive.

a) It would be foolish if one believed his promise.

b) It is dangerous if you cross the street during the rush-hour.

c) It is wrong if you judge people by their appearance.

d) It is crazy if one goes out in this terrible weather.

e) It was strange when you saw his behaviour.

f) It is difficult if you learn a foreign language without any help.

g) It is clever if one compares prices in different shops before buying something.

h) It is disappointing when you get bad marks in a test you worked hard for.

i) It is not as simple as it looks if you learn inline-skating.

j) It is sad when you see how nature is polluted.

Aufgabe 9 Complete the dialogue with the appropriate expressions.

PAM: When does John arrive?
BOB: John _____. (wahrscheinlich um 20 Uhr)
PAM: Is he coming by car?
BOB: He _____ because it broke down yesterday. (wahrscheinlich nicht)
PAM: Will he be on time?
BOB: John _____ on time, he's always punctual. (sicherlich)

- Der Infinitiv mit *to* **nach Nomen**: Der Infinitiv mit *to* kann nach Nomen **anstelle eines Relativsatzes mit modalem Hilfsverb** stehen. Folgt auf das Verb eine Präposition, so steht sie im Satz mit Infinitiv an der gleichen Stelle, an der sie auch im Relativsatz steht.
  Beispiele: This doctor is the right man who can help you.
  This doctor is the right man to help you.
  This is a new record that you should listen to.
  This is a new record to listen to.
- Ebenso kann ein Infinitiv mit *to* nach *somebody, something* usw. anstelle eines nachfolgenden Relativsatzes mit Modalverb stehen.
  Beispiele: Here's something that must be done.
  Here's something to be done.

Aufgabe 10 Rewrite the sentences using an infinitive.

a) If Carol had a friend she could go out with, she would be happier.
   _____

b) She says she can't go to the dinner party because she hasn't anything she can wear.
   _____

c) We'd like to have a house in the country in which we could live closer to nature.
   _____

d) Haven't you got anything we could open the bottle with?
   _____

e) This is a dentist you can trust.
   _____

f) They bought an old house which should be renovated.
_____

g) I don't know anybody who could take care of your dog when you are on holiday.
_____

h) We need somebody who can repair our computer.
_____

> - Wenn die Infinitivkonstruktion ein **eigenes Sinnsubjekt** hat, so wird dieses häufig durch die Präposition *for* eingeleitet. Nach *for* folgt dann also ein Nomen oder ein Pronomen. Diese Struktur (*for* + Nomen/Pronomen + *to*-Infinitiv) kann auf ein Nomen oder ein Adjektiv folgen. Das Adjektiv ist dabei oft durch *too* oder *enough* näher bestimmt.
>   *Beispiele:* This is a book <u>for Helen</u> <u>to read</u> on the train.
>   This suitcase is <u>too heavy</u> <u>for you</u> <u>to carry</u>.

Aufgabe 11 Glimpses of Life in the US: Complete the sentences with *for* + infinitive.

a) It is common (Americans pay) _____ a baby-sitter to look after their children in the evening.

b) It is normal (teenage girls and boys work) _____ as baby-sitters.

c) It is usual (Americans shake) _____ hands when they meet someone for the first time.

d) Aerobic exercises are an ideal sport (Americans keep) _____ fit.

e) It is important (many Americans stay) _____ in good shape.

f) Today about 20 million Hispanics live in the US. (Many of them) _____ English is too difficult (learn) _____, so they keep speaking Spanish.

g) It is not easy (foreigners understand) _____ American English. For example they say "I'm gonna" instead of "I'm going to".

h) It is more common (Americans use) _____ computers for education than it is in Europe.

i) As they work a lot, it is necessary (Americans plan) _____ their leisure time carefully.

j) It is customary (Americans celebrate) _____ Thanksgiving with big dinners and family reunions.

Aufgabe 12 Talking About Law Breakers: Combine the sentences by using *too, enough* + infinitive.

a) There weren't many fingerprints. The police couldn't detect the thief.
_____

b) In some parts of American cities there is very much violence. The police can't cope with it.
_____

c) Today there is intensive cooperation between the police in European countries. Terrorists can't escape.
_____

d) Many people say that our laws are not severe. Criminals are not deterred by them.
_____

e) In the US lie detectors are considered to be very useful. The police should employ them more often.
_____

f) Capital punishment by the electric chair is extremely cruel. Even murderers should not be killed by these means.
_____

g) Hooliganism is very dangerous. Society should not make light of it.
_____

h) The fine is very high. The smuggler can't pay it.
_____

i) The number of crimes is very high. The police can't arrest all the lawbreakers.
_____

> - Der Infinitiv mit *to* **nach Fragewörtern**: Nach Fragewörtern *(when, where, what* usw.) kann der Infinitiv **anstelle eines Nebensatzes mit modalem Hilfsverb** *(can, must, should* usw.) stehen.
>   *Beispiel:* I didn't know <u>what I should do</u>.
>   I didn't know <u>what</u> <u>to do.</u>

Aufgabe 13 The Pilgrim Fathers: Rewrite the sentences using an infinitive.

a) They did not know where they should settle down.

b) They did not know which corn they should cultivate.

c) They had no idea how they should survive the first winter.

d) They asked the Indians how they should use bows and arrows.

e) They wondered how they should grow vegetables different from the English ones, such as pumpkins or potatoes.

f) They did not know how they could build wooden houses without nails.

g) They were at a loss to know at what time of the year they should plant seeds on the ground.

h) They had no idea how they could fertilize their plants.

i) They asked the Indians where they could find wild fruits and mushrooms.

j) When the Pilgrim Fathers had become successful farmers, they decided how they should celebrate the first Thanksgiving.

- Der Infinitiv mit *to* nach **Superlativen, Ordinalzahlen** und *the only*: Der Infinitiv mit *to* wird nach Superlativen, Ordinalzahlen und *the only* **anstelle eines Relativsatzes** verwendet.

    Beispiele: This is the best thing that one can do.
    This is the best thing to do.
    My girlfriend was the first who arrived.
    My girlfriend was the first to arrive.
    Mr Parker is the only person who can help us.
    Mr Parker is the only person to help us.

Aufgabe 14 Space travel: Form sentences using an infinitive.

a) It was one of the most bitter experiences for the American nation – realize that the Soviet Union was the first – launch a satellite, the Sputnik, into orbit in 1957.

b) Yuri Gagarin – first man – travel in space – in 1961.

c) First American – orbit the Earth – John Glenn – in 1962.

d) Apollo 11 – only spaceship – land on the lunar Sea of Tranquility – in 1969.

e) "Challenger" – only space shuttle – explode – in 1986.

f) The most expensive space programme – land on Mars was started in 1995.

g) Most people considered – it – be absurd – land on Mars.

h) "Sojourner" a car-like vehicle – first man-made object – land on Mars in 1997.

i) The most famous science fiction series – be seen on TV – Star Trek.

Aufgabe 15*

Mixed exercise: Bill Gates – Microsoft's boss of bosses. Complete the sentences with the correct form of the English words.

machen	Bill Gates' aim was _____ computers better and easier
benutzen	_____. He was the first _____ a monopoly of
aufbauen	software with "Windows". Once he was asked "How does it feel
sein	_____ a boss?"; and he answered: "A boss always ought
leisten	to _____ a good job." It is one of the most important
herausfinden	things for him _____ his customers' demands,
vorhersagen	otherwise he says, it is impossible _____ Microsoft's
leiten	future. Today he is the richest man in the world _____
erfinden	a business. It is his dream _____ the "easy-to-use"
integrieren	computer. It is vitally important for him _____ the
	Internet completely into his software. Many Americans are of the
	opinion that Bill Gates' monopoly is too powerful for other
konkurrieren	companies _____ with, they say that the US govern-
brechen	ment had better _____ his monopoly. Critics advise the
lassen	US president not _____ him _____ too powerful,
werden	otherwise Bill Gates would _____ all of America's econo-
beeinflussen	my.

8.2 Gerundium oder Infinitiv?

> Auf eine Reihe von **Verben und Wendungen** kann ein Gerundium *oder* ein Infinitiv folgen. Dabei musst du beachten, dass sich in vielen Fällen die Bedeutung des Verbs ändern kann.
>
> *Beispiel:* John stopped <u>smoking</u>.
> (John hörte auf zu rauchen.)
>
> Peter stopped <u>to smoke</u>.
> (Peter hörte auf [mit irgendeiner Tätigkeit], um zu rauchen.)

- Einige wenige Verben **behalten ihre Bedeutung bei**, ganz gleich, ob ihnen ein Gerundium oder ein Infinitiv folgt. Zu diesen Verben gehören *to begin, to start, to continue, to intend*.
  Beispiel: The Beatles began to play / playing at beat clubs.

- **Bedeutungsänderungen** bei nachfolgendem Infinitiv bzw. Gerundium: Nach den Verben *like, love, hate* und *prefer* verwendet man das Gerundium, wenn man eine allgemeine, immer gültige Aussage machen will. Man verwendet nach diesen Verben jedoch den Infinitiv, wenn man sich auf eine konkrete Situation oder einen bestimmten Einzelfall bezieht. Auf die Konditionalformen *I'd like* und *I'd love* folgt immer der Infinitiv.
  Beispiele: I hate listening to pop music.
  I loved to listen to the Beatles' evergreens at your party.

Aufgabe 16   The Beatles come to Germany: Complete with the infinitive or gerund.

Which of the early Beatles' songs would you like _____ (listen to)? In 1963, the Beatles' fourth single "She Loves You" started _____ (conquer) most European countries. German youngsters loved _____ (imitate) the Anglo-American lifestyle. In 1962, the Beatles preferred _____ (make) guest appearances at the "Star Club" in Hamburg. For several years German teenagers loved _____ (have) the "mophead" hairstyle of the Beatles. "Yeah, yeah, yeah", the refrain of "She Loves You", was very often broadcasted. Adults hated _____ (hear) it around the clock. The Beatles' music was a shock for people who love _____ (listen to) classical music.

- *used to* mit Gerundium oder Infinitiv: *used to* **mit Gerundium** bedeutet ‚etwas zu tun gewöhnt sein'. *used to* **mit Infinitiv** bedeutet, dass früher einmal eine Handlung stattfand, die in der Gegenwart nicht mehr andauert. Von *used to* gibt es nur das *past tense* mit den Formen *used to, (he) did use* und *(he) didn't use*.
  Beispiele: I'm used to working with the radio on.
  (Ich bin daran gewöhnt, bei Radiomusik zu arbeiten.)
  When my dad was younger, he used to play soccer.
  (Als mein Vater jung war, spielte er Fußball.)

- *remember* und *forget* mit Gerundium oder Infinitiv: Wenn auf diese beiden Verben ein **Infinitiv** folgt, so bedeutet dies, dass etwas in der Zukunft geschehen soll oder muss. Folgt jedoch ein **Gerundium**, so bezieht sich die Handlung auf die Vergangenheit.
  Beispiele: I must remember to post the letter.
  (Ich muss daran denken, den Brief aufzugeben.)
  I don't remember posting the letter.
  (Ich erinnere mich nicht daran, dass ich den Brief schon aufgegeben habe.)

... rund ums Verb: Infinitiv

> - *mean* mit Gerundium oder Infinitiv: *mean* mit nachfolgendem **Infinitiv** bedeutet ‚beabsichtigen, vorhaben'. *mean* mit nachfolgendem **Gerundium** heißt ‚beinhalten, bedeuten'.
>
>   Beispiele: I <u>mean to work</u> harder.
>   (Ich beabsichtige, härter zu arbeiten.)
>   Our train leaves at 6 p.m., that <u>means getting up</u> early.
>   (Unser Zug fährt um 6 Uhr, das bedeutet, dass wir früh aufstehen müssen.)

Aufgabe 17 Gerund or infinitive? Complete the sentences.

a) Mrs Baxter works for a computer company. She programmes software for doctors which means (have) _____ special knowledge of medical problems. Her daughter means (specialize) _____ in this subject, too.

b) Mr Webson is a stockbroker. He is used (work) _____ in the noisy London stock exchange. He used (work) _____ in a bank before he took up (buy and sell) _____ stocks.

c) Can you lend me some 50 pence stamps? I always forget (buy) _____ stamps when I am at the post office. – Yes, of course. I've got three in my purse, although I don't remember (buy) _____ them.

d) Are you sure you didn't forget to switch off the lights? – Quite sure. I remember (switch) _____ them off before I left the flat.

e) When the racing car came nearer, I stopped (watch) _____ it. – You mean you stopped (work) _____ just because of a racing car?

f) I hate (swim) _____ in swimming pools, but last summer, when we were on holiday, the sea was rather cold. So we preferred (swim) _____ in the hotel swimming pool.

g) Due to bad weather conditions, my flight was cancelled. That meant (wait) _____ for five hours for the next flight.

h) I'll never forget (hear) _____ her singing.

i) I must not forget (send) _____ a fax to the hotel before our departure.

j) She's looking forward (meet) _____ him again. She'll be really happy (see) _____ him after such a long time.

k) You ought (drink) _____ less coffee. – Yes, I know, but I'm used (drink) _____ three cups a day, and I find it hard (give up) _____ (drink) _____ coffee.

… rund ums Verb: Infinitiv

Aufgabe 18 British-German sporting relations: Combine the sentences using gerund or infinitive. Fill in the missing prepositions if necessary.

Tennis: Wimbledon

a) In the 90s Wimbledon spectators watched fantastic tennis with German players. They enjoyed it.

b) Boris Becker and Steffi Graf made German tennis world-famous. They won the World Championships repeatedly.

c) In 1985, Boris Becker won Wimbledon. Seventeen-year-old Becker was the youngest player.

d) In 1988 Steffi Graf succeeded. She won the women's title.

Soccer: The "Wembley Goal"

e) In 1966 the German soccer team lost the World Cup final in Wembley Stadium. German fans and a lot of British spectators denied it. They said the third goal was not a goal.

f) The referee gave the goal good. He insisted on it.

g) The German team did not accept the referee's decision. They refused it.

h) The English team won the World Cup. The team was very lucky.

Car racing

i) Michael Schumacher won the Formula I World Racing Championships in 1994 for the first time. He relied on a car made by British engineers.

_____
_____

j) Today, Michael Schumacher doesn't race for British Benetton. He races for the Italian Ferrari company instead.

_____
_____

Aufgabe 19 Find the nouns corresponding to the following words.

speak	_____	grow	_____
necessary	_____	advertise	_____
prefer	_____	fail	_____
sit	_____	succeed	_____
arrive	_____	warn	_____

Aufgabe 20 Fill in the silent letters. Rewrite the correct words.

fas__en, a pair of s__issors, no dou__t, ca__m, g__ost, the king's rei__n, thum__

Aufgabe 21 Homophones (words with the same pronounciation) and different spellings and meanings. Find the corresponding homophones.

steal	_____	week	_____
part	_____	lose	_____
waste	_____	principal	_____
flea	_____	through	_____
sight	_____	night	_____

… rund um den Satz

9 Indirekte Rede

Mit der indirekten Rede *(reported speech)* kannst du Äußerungen wiedergeben. Du kannst also über etwas berichten, das gesagt wurde.

Beispiel: Tom said: "I am hungry."   *(direct speech)*
              Tom said that he was hungry.   *(reported speech)*

Was musst du beachten, wenn du Sätze in der indirekten Rede bildest?

Die indirekte Rede wird durch Verben wie *say, tell, answer, ask* eingeleitet, an die sich ein *that*-Satz anschließt. Die Konjunktion *that* ist dabei fakultativ, kann also auch weggelassen werden.

Wenn du eine Aussage, die in der direkten Rede steht, in die indirekte Rede umformen willst, so musst du folgende Regeln beachten:

- Steht das Verb, das die indirekte Rede einleitet, im *present tense, present perfect* oder *will-future*, so bleibt die **Zeitform**, die das Verb in der direkten Rede aufweist, in der indirekten Rede **unverändert**:

  Beispiele: John says: "I want to become a vet."
               John says that he wants to become a vet.

               John has recently said: "I want to become a vet."
               John has recently said that he wants to become a vet.

               John will tell you: "I want to become a vet."
               John will tell you that he wants to become a vet.

- Die Zeiten in der indirekten Rede werden ebenfalls **nicht verändert**, wenn die Aussage **allgemein gültig** ist oder wenn die Aussage zum Zeitpunkt des Sprechens **noch zutrifft**:

  Beispiele: Tony said: "London is bigger than Munich."
               Tony said that London is bigger than Munich.
               Ben said: "I am bad at French."
               Ben said that he is bad at French.

... rund um den Satz: Indirekte Rede

- Wenn das Verb, das die indirekte Rede einleitet, jedoch in einer Zeitform der Vergangenheit steht, so musst du die **Zeiten** in der indirekten Rede **wie folgt umformen:**

Direkte Rede		Indirekte Rede
simple present	→	simple past
present continuous	→	past continuous
simple past	→	past perfect
past continuous	→	past perfect continuous
present perfect	→	past perfect
present perfect continuous	→	past perfect continuous
past perfect	=	past perfect
will-future	→	would + infinitiv
going to-future	→	was/were going to + infinitve

Beispiel: Tom said: "I am going to Spain soon."
Tom said that he was going to Spain soon.

Aufgabe 1 Sue Thomas met Greg Webb, the well-known racing driver, at a disco. He told her a lot of things about himself. What does Sue tell her friend at school the next day? Change Greg's words *(direct speech)* into what Sue tells her friend *(reported speech)*.

a) "I'm a racing driver."
   He said he _____

b) "I've been racing for just over a year."
   _____

c) "I've won a lot of races."
   _____

d) "I live a dangerous life!"
   _____

e) "I'm going to buy a new Rolls Royce, because I crashed my old one."
   _____

f) "My next race will be in Monte Carlo."
   _____

g) "I'll take you with me if you want."
   _____

> - **Personal- und Possessivpronomen:** Ebenfalls verändert werden die Personal- und Possessivpronomen der 1. und 2. Person Singular und Plural:
>   Beispiel: He said: "My brother will stay with <u>us</u>."
>   He said <u>his</u> brother would stay with <u>them</u>.
> - Die **Demonstrativpronomen** *this, these* werden zu *that, those*:
>   Beispiel: He said: "I like <u>this</u> place."
>   He said he liked <u>that</u> place.
> - **Adverbien:** Ort- und Zeitadverbien werden wie folgt verändert:
>
> | Direkte Rede | | Indirekte Rede |
> |---|---|---|
> | here | → | there |
> | today | → | that day |
> | yesterday | → | the day before |
> | one hour ago | → | one hour before |
> | last week/month etc. | → | the week/month before – the previous week/month |
> | tomorrow | → | the next/following day |
> | next week etc. | → | the following week |
> | the day before yesterday | → | two days before |
> | the day after tomorrow | → | in two days time |
>
> Beispiele: He said: "It's quite nice <u>here</u>."
> He said it was quite nice <u>there</u>.
>
> She said: "I'll come back <u>tomorrow</u>."
> She said she would come back the <u>next/following day</u>.

Aufgabe 2 Answer the questions at the end of each situation using reported speech.

a) "Our prices are very low", were the words you read in an advertisement. Why did you go to that shop?
Because the advertisement said _____

b) "I know the way", your friend said when you went for a walk with him and got lost.
Why didn't you turn back?
_____

c) Richard asked his teacher about his mark in the English test. The teacher's answer was: "Your mark is very good and I've noticed a big improvement in your English."
Why was Richard smiling when he came out of the English lesson?
_____

... rund um den Satz: Indirekte Rede

d) When Kelly's boyfriend phoned she told him: "My German teacher has given us so much homework that I'll probably take all evening to finish it!"
Why didn't Kelly go out with her boyfriend?

e) You met a friend on the way to school. He said: "My mountain bike has been stolen."
Why did your friend go to school on foot?

f) Ray is in your class at school. He wasn't there yesterday. When you phoned him after school he said: "I'm ill in bed with a high temperature."
The same afternoon you saw Ray looking completely healthy and holding a tennis racquet.
Why were you surprised?

g) Mr and Mrs Hope invited the new next-door-neighbours to dinner. They accepted but said: "We're vegetarians."
Why did Mrs Hope cook a meal without any meat?

h) Frank made arrangements with his girlfriend Rebecca. He said: "I'll meet you in front of the cinema at 7.30." At 8.15 Rebecca was still standing in front of the cinema, waiting.
Why was she angry with her boyfriend?

Aufgabe 3   Michael J., the famous pop star has arrived in Germany for a two-week concert tour. Here are some of the things he said during a press conference. Write what Michael said:

a) "I feel great because my wife and son are going to join me tomorrow."

b) "I arrived at Munich airport three hours ago."

... rund um den Satz: Indirekte Rede ❘ 111

c) "My first concert will be next Saturday, in Munich. Yesterday I was in Hamburg. The fans were great there."

d) "My wife and son will accompany me for the next two weeks."

e) "My son's doing fine. He began to walk two weeks ago. We're looking forward to having another baby next year and we'd like a girl."

f) "While we're in Germany, were going to buy a little old castle somewhere on top of a mountain. We need a place where we can just relax and enjoy a normal family life."

g) "I really enjoy being a father but I don't see my son very often. The last time I saw him was three weeks ago, that's why I've brought my family to Germany."

h) "I'm feeling fine. I had a bad cold last week and I lost my voice but I'm OK again. I just have to be careful that I don't get too close to anyone. If I go down with another cold I'll be forced to cancel the tour."

i) We're going to do a sound check in the Olympia Concert Hall tomorrow afternoon.

j) "It's fantastic to be in little old Germany again and I love you all!"

> - Auch **Hilfsverben** musst du wie folgt abändern:
>
> | Direkte Rede | | Indirekte Rede |
> |---|---|---|
> | may | → | might |
> | can | → | could |
> | must | → | had to (Notwendigkeit) |
> | must | → | must (Annahme) |
>
> Beispiel: Tom asked: "<u>Can</u> I stay home today?"
> Tom asked if he <u>could</u> stay home that day.
>
> Außerdem kann *needn't* durch *didn't have to* und *mustn't* durch *wasn't/ weren't to* ersetzt werden.
>
> Beispiele: He said to me: "You <u>needn't</u> do it."
> He said I <u>needn't</u> do it./He said I <u>didn't have to</u> do it.
> He said: "You <u>mustn't</u> sleep too long."
> He said I <u>mustn't</u> sleep too long./He said I <u>wasn't to</u> sleep too long..

Aufgabe 4 David Green, is a member of the Society for the Promotion of Nature Conservation. He has been invited to speak to the local conservationist group. You were at the meeting and are now telling a friend what David said.

a) We believe that more people should be aware of how many plants and wild flowers are becoming rare or dying out.

b) Many flowers and plants which used to grow in the countryside in the 19th century are now unknown.

c) We ought to do something soon because more and more species of wild animals will become extinct.

d) The fines for dumping waste in rivers must be so high that companies will no longer prefer to pay them instead of investing in recycling.

... rund um den Satz: Indirekte Rede 113

e) If we don't act now, it may be too late to save our planet.

f) We mustn't shut our eyes to the misuse of the environment.

g) The millions of dollars which governments spend on defence could be invested in protecting our environment.

h) We have to put more pressure on the politicians.

i) We should encourage our children to take care of the planet Earth.

j) We can't go on polluting our environment and thinking we needn't worry about the consequences.

> **Wie kannst du verschiedene Sprechabsichten in der indirekten Rede verwirklichen?**
> Sprechabsichten können in der indirekte Rede mit passenden Verben ausgedrückt werden:
> **Vorschläge:** *to suggest doing sth.*
> **Einladungen** und **Angebote:** *to invite, to offer to do sth.*
> **Bitten:** *to ask*
> **Ratschläge:** *to advise s.o. to do sth.*
> **Befehle:** *to tell s.o. to do sth.*
> *Beispiel:* Tom: "Shall we play tennis?"
> Tom <u>suggested</u> playing tennis.

Aufgabe 5 Some members of the audience asked David how we could help to protect the environment. Change his answers into reported speech using appropriate verbs.

a) "Put glass, tin and plastic into the special containers."

b) "Why don't you use your bikes or go on foot more often?"

c) "Would you like to come to an information evening next Friday?"

d) "Shall I give you more information on recycling?"

e) "Please set a good example by not leaving rubbish on the beach or in the countryside."

f) "Don't use your cars so often!"

g) "You'd better save energy by switching off unnecessary lights."

h) "Won't you have one of my booklets, 'Friends of the Earth'?"

i) "Please join 'Friends of the Earth' or 'Greenpeace'."

j) "Would you put some money in the box on your way out?"

k) "Would you like to join me for some organically-grown refreshments in the foyer?"

Wie bildest du Fragen in der indirekten Rede?

- Fragen in der indirekten Rede leitest du zumeist mit *ask, want to know, enquire* usw. ein. Für die indirekten Fragen gelten die **gleichen Regeln** bezüglich der Zeitenverschiebung, der Pronomen und der adverbialen Bestimmungen wie für die indirekten Aussagesätze:

  Beispiel: Pam asked Jill: "How long have you been learning English at this school?"
  Pam asked Jill how long she had been learning English at that school.

- Wenn in der direkten Rede kein Fragewort steht, muss die Frage in der indirekten Rede mit *if* oder *whether* eingeleitet werden:

  Beispiel: Ben to Bob: "Did you manage to catch the train?"
  Ben wanted to know if Bob had managed to catch the train.

Aufgabe 6 Katie Harrison has applied for a holiday job in the USA. She wants to work in an American summer camp, looking after groups of school children. After the interview she tells her mother what the interviewer, Ray Carter, asked her. Put his questions into reported speech.

a) "Could you tell me how old you are?"
He asked me _____

b) "Have you ever had any experience of working with 10 to 11 year-olds?"
He wanted to know _____

c) "Do you think you might have any problems speaking English all the time?"
He enquired _____

d) "Do you speak any other languages?"
_____

e) "How long could you stay in the USA?"
_____

f) "Have you got any friends or relatives in America?"
_____

g) "Is there any particular area of the USA that you would like to go to?"
_____

h) "Why do you want to work in the USA?"
_____

i) "Is this the first time that you've applied for a job like this?"
_____

j) "Could you imagine having problems with homesickness?"
_____

k) "Would your parents be prepared to give me their agreement in writing?"
_____

l) "Shall I give you some more information about the sort of things you would be expected to do?"
_____

... rund um den Satz: Indirekte Rede

m) "Are you aware that once you have signed this contract it will no longer be possible for you to change your mind?"

n) "Did you receive the summer camp brochures we sent you last week?"

o) "Are you able to pay for the return flight to the USA yourself?"

p) "What is the earliest date you could fly?"

q) "Is there anything else you would like to ask me about the job?"

r) "Would you mind giving me one or two days to consider your application before I let you know my decision?"

Aufgabe 7* Mixed exercise: Here is part of an interview between Jennifer Palmer, a journalist and Peter Cook, who has just written a book called: 'Television? No Thank you!' Put Jennifer's questions and Peter's answers into reported speech. Use as many different ways of beginning the reported questions and statements as possible.

a) JENNIFER: Why are you so against television?

b) PETER: I think that television is partly responsible for the break-up of family life.

c) JENNIFER: How much time does the average person spend watching television?

d) PETER: According to the latest statistics. between four in the afternoon and midnight, at least 12 million viewers are sure to be watching television. This figure can rise to 37 million at peak viewing hours.

e) JENNIFER: Can you suggest some things people could do instead of watching TV?

f) PETER: Why not go to the cinema or the theatre?

g) JENNIFER: Why do so many people spend their evenings in front of the television?

h) PETER: The main reason must be laziness! It's so easy just to switch on the TV. Unfortunately, a lot of people just leave it on even if they are not interested in the programme.

i) JENNIFER: I'm worried about the negative effect TV could have on my children. Can you give me some advice?

j) PETER: If I were you I would choose the programmes your children watch very carefully. You should also sit with them while they are watching in case they have any questions.

k) JENNIFER: I often switch on the TV to relax after a long day at work. Should I get rid of my television?

l) PETER: You needn't get rid of your television. If I were you, I would take up a sport or hobby which you could do in the evenings.

m) JENNIFER: Is there anything else you would like to say?

n) PETER: There is more to life than sitting in front of a box. Don't let television take over your lives!

o) JENNIFER: It's been very enjoyable talking to you. Would you like to join me for a coffee?

... rund um den Satz: Indirekte Rede

p) PETER: I'm sorry but I haven't got time for a coffee. I must go home immediately because there's a programme on TV that I would like to watch. Why don't we have a coffee together tomorrow?

Aufgabe 8 Word formation: Complete the verbs using prefixes.

		m	i	t	= to leave out
		m	i	t	= to do sth. wrong, bad, unlawful
		m	i	t	= to agree to obey

	c	e	i	v	e	= to get sth. given or sent
	c	e	i	v	e	= to cause sb. to believe sth. that is false
	c	e	i	v	e	= to see, to hear
	c	e	i	v	e	= to imagine, to think of

---

s-Genitiv

- singular noun + 's
  Beispiel: my father's car

- plural noun + '
  Beispiel: her parents' home

- irregular plural + 's
  Beispiel: the children's mother

Aufgabe 9 Complete the expressions.

the Smith__ children, in a week__ time, a children__ book, Jeff and Jill__ dog, James__ friends, the boss__ office, a friend of Alice__, a cousin of John__, the women__ dresses, the ladies__ hats

10 Relativsätze

Relativsätze haben die Funktion, ein Nomen oder ein Pronomen des Hauptsatzes näher zu charakterisieren. Du leitest sie mit Relativpronomen *(relative pronouns)* ein.

Wie verwendest du Relativpronomen?
- Wenn das Relativpronomen im Relativsatz die Funktion des **Subjektes** einnimmt, so lautet es für **Personen** *who* oder *that*, für **Sachen** *which* oder *that*.
  Beispiele: This is the lady who/that helped me.
  Where is the pen which/that I lent you?
- Wenn das Relativpronomen im Relativsatz die Funktion des **Objektes** einnimmt, so lautet es für **Personen** in der Umgangssprache *who* oder *that*, in der Schriftsprache *whom*. Für **Sachen** verwendet man *which* oder *that*.
  Beispiele: The boy whom/who/that you saw yesterday is Italian.
  The film which/that we saw was interesting.
- Wenn mit dem Relativpronomen eine Zugehörigkeit ausgedrückt werden soll, so hat es die Form *whose* (= dessen): *whose* kann für **Personen und Sachen** verwendet werden.
  Beispiele: The boy whose father is an engineer is called Ben.
  The house whose windows are broken is for sale.

Aufgabe 1 Combine the sentences using a relative pronoun.

a) This man is a Pakistani.   He has a British passport.

___

b) This girl is Indian.   Her passport is blue.

___

c) Swansea has racial minorities.   It's a trading centre.

___

… rund um den Satz: Relativsätze

> **Welche Arten von Relativsätzen gibt es?**
>
> - Man unterscheidet zwischen **bestimmenden** und **nicht bestimmenden Relativsätzen**. Wenn der Relativsatz notwendig ist, um klar zu machen, welche Sache bzw. Person gemeint ist, so ist er „bestimmend". Wenn der Relativsatz jedoch lediglich eine zusätzliche Information gibt, so ist er „nicht bestimmend". Nicht bestimmende Relativsätze werden durch Kommas vom Hauptsatz getrennt.
>   *Beispiele:* Do you know the man who is talking to Mary? (bestimmender Relativsatz)
>   The Pope, who is of Polish origin, travels a lot. (nicht bestimmender Relativsatz)
>
> - In einigen Fällen kannst du Relativsätze bilden, **ohne ein Relativpronomen** zu verwenden. Du kannst das Relativpronomen dann weglassen, wenn es als Objekt in einem bestimmenden Relativsatz verwendet wird. Man bezeichnet Relativsätze ohne Relativpronomen als *contact clauses*.
>   *Beispiel:* The boy you saw yesterday won a prize.

Aufgabe 2 Combine the sentences by forming *contact clauses*.

a) The girl comes from Sri Lanka.   I met her on the boat.

_____

b) The gentleman lives in Zimbabwe.   You can see him over there.

_____

c) The jobs are not desirable.   They want to have the jobs.

_____

d) These Asians are from Burma.   They are waiting for permission to immigrate.

_____

> **An welche Stelle im Relativsatz stellst du die Präposition?**
>
> Wenn in einem Relativsatz ein Verb mit einer dazugehörigen Präposition auftaucht, so steht die **Präposition** in der **Umgangssprache am Satzende**. In der **Schriftsprache** steht die **Präposition vor whom** bzw. *which*.
>
> *Beispiel:* This is the man (that) I told you about.
> This is the man about whom I told you.

... rund um den Satz: Relativsätze 121

Aufgabe 3 Combine the sentences by forming *contact clauses*. Be careful about where you put the preposition. Write in formal style.

a) The problems are serious.
   We were talking about the problems.
   _____

b) The lady works in an immigration office.
   You are looking at her.
   _____

c) The waiter comes from the West Indies.
   I always forget the name of this waiter.
   _____

d) The new law restricts immigration.
   You have heard about the new law.
   _____

e) The speech was about Kenya's independence.
   We listened to the speech.
   _____

f) The advantages are part of the welfare system.
   They are entitled to those advantages.
   _____

g) This was their last chance to immigrate.
   They were waiting for this chance.
   _____

h) The immigration figures are high.
   Britain is faced with these immigration figures.
   _____

Aufgabe 4* Mixed exercise – Hawaii: Complete the sentences.

Hawaii, _____ has been called the "little US", became the 50th state in 1959. This state consists of 132 islands, _____ the island of Hawaii is the biggest and the most important. Before the Japanese attack at Pearl Harbour on December 7, 1941, _____ drew the US into World

... rund um den Satz: Relativsätze

War II, the islands were almost unknown to most of the world. The natives, _____ land had been taken by American farmers _____ grew sugar cane and pineapples, were decimated by disease, such as small pox, _____ was introduced by outsiders. Due to tourism, the state's population has increased. Lots of people _____ jobs are provided by tourism earn a living there. Some native Hawaiians _____ private land has been taken over by big US companies try to fight against foreign denomination – in vain. Most Hawaiians, _____ outlook on the future is optimistic, believe in an equal-opportunity society. They welcome foreigners with the friendly "aloha", _____ means "love".

Aufgabe 5 Word formation: Fill in the missing words.

Verb	Noun	Adjective
attract		
	fear	
	vitality	
		original
	destruction	
		different
pride (oneself upon)		
	reliance	
invent		
	fascination	

11 Sprechabsichten

Um bestimmte Sachverhalte, z. B. Ursache und Wirkung, Bedingungen oder Einschränkungen ausdrücken zu können, brauchst du das geeignete sprachliche Handwerkszeug. Das folgende Kapitel hilft dir dabei, deine mündliche und schriftliche Ausdrucksfähigkeit im Bereich der Sprechabsichten zu verbessern.

Wie drückst du Vergleiche aus?

- It ... such a ... that ... oder ... so ... that ...
  Beispiele: It was such a good drink that I had two glasses.
  The drink was so good that I had two glasses.
- No ... + comparative + than ...
  Beispiel: No hotel is more comfortable than the "Red Lion".
- The + comparative ..., the + comparative ...
  Beispiel: The more you work, the more money you have.

Aufgabe 1 Form comparative sentences with *It ... such a ... that* and *... so ... that ...*

a) film / boring – I nearly fell asleep.

b) car / expensive – I can't buy it.

c) book / bad – I can't read it.

Aufgabe 2 Form comparative sentences using *No ... + comparative + than.*

a) Japan / exports cars – any other country.

b) A Chevrolet / consumes petrol – any other car.

c) A Volvo / safe – any other car.

... rund um den Satz: Sprechabsichten

Aufgabe 3 Form comparative sentences with *The* + comparative, *the* + comparative.

a) We stayed in London (long) – we liked the city.
___

b) You eat (little) – you weigh (little).
___

c) One practises (more) – one plays an instrument (well).
___

> **Wie drückst du Bedingungen aus?**
> - *If + present tense + future*: Dieser Satztyp drückt eine **offene Bedingung** aus, d. h. die Bedingung kann erfüllt werden. Sobald sie erfüllt ist, folgt die jeweilige Handlung.
>   Beispiel: If I have enough money, I will buy a car.
> - *If + past tense + conditional I*: Dieser Satztyp drückt aus, dass die **Bedingung** zum Zeitpunkt des Sprechens **nicht erfüllt ist**, deshalb muss die Handlung unterbleiben.
>   Beispiel: If I had money, I would buy a car.
> - *If + past perfect + conditional II*: Dieser Satztyp drückt aus, dass die **Bedingung** in der Vergangenheit **nicht erfüllt war** und dass die Handlung deshalb unterbleiben musste.
>   Beispiel: If I had had money, I would have bought a car.

Aufgabe 4 In London: Complete the sentences.

a) If you came to London, you _____ (find) lots of shopping centres.
b) If you _____ (want to buy) antiques, you'll find these things in Bond Street.
c) If you _____ (to be interested in) teenage fashion, you'll have to go to Carnaby Street.
d) If you had visited the Tower, you _____ (see) the Wardens and the ravens.
e) If the weather _____ (be fine), we would lie in a deck chair in Hyde Park.
f) You could have spent a week more, if you _____ (save) more money.

Aufgabe 5 Holidays: Use the correct tenses of the given verbs.

JANE: If I _____ (be) you, Sarah, I _____ (go) to Scotland for my holiday.
SARAH: Of course, I _____ (like) to come with you, If I _____ (have) the money.
JANE: If you _____ (not buy) so many computer games, you _____ (can easily join) us.
SARAH: You're right. Which guidebook _____ (you recommend), if I _____ (want) detailed information about Scotland?
JANE: If you _____ (be) really interested, I _____ (lend) you my guidebook.

Aufgabe 6 Form conditional sentences using the appropriate type of conditional.

a) Open the door, or I won't be able to come in.

b) She must wear sunglasses because her eyes ache.

c) Remind me about Bill's birthday or I won't send him a birthday card.

d) She feels terrible because she has a test tomorrow.

e) Tom didn't revise for the test and so he failed.

f) His parents didn't give him the money so he couldn't buy the interrail ticket.

Wie drückst du eine Absicht aus?

- ... in order (not) to ...
  Beispiel: I got up early <u>in order to</u> catch the train.

Wie drückst du eine Ursache und das darauf folgende Ergebnis aus?

- as/since ..., + Ergebnis
  Beispiel: <u>As/Since</u> it was raining, we didn't go for a walk.
- The reason why ... + result
  Beispiel: <u>The reason why</u> we didn't go for a walk was the rain.

Wie drückst du ein Zugeständnis aus?

- although + Nebensatz + Hauptsatz
  Beispiel: <u>Although</u> the weather was bad, we went to the beach.
- in spite of + nominale Wendung + Hauptsatz
  Beispiel: <u>In spite of</u> all his money, he isn't happy.

Aufgabe 7 Join the two sentences expressing the idea of 'intention'.
a) I'll work longer this week. I want to have a day off next week.

b) They spoke quietly. They didn't want to wake the baby.

c) Read the text twice. You'll understand it better.

d) He carried the vase carefully. He didn't want to break it.

Aufgabe 8 Join the two sentences. Express the idea of 'cause and result' in two different ways.
a) Tom stayed in bed. He felt ill.

b) He didn't get the job. He was not qualified for it.

c) The worker was sacked. He didn't work carefully.

d) I carried her bag for her. It was very heavy.

Aufgabe 9 Complete the sentences using *although* or *in spite of*.
a) We went to the beach _____ the bad weather.
b) _____ it was raining all afternoon, the competition took place as planned.
c) _____ we were very tired, we went to the museum.
d) We enjoyed the walk _____ the rain.

Aufgabe 10 Join the two sentences using *although* or *in spite of*.

a) They don't have much money. – They want to have a new car.

b) She walked quickly. – Her suitcase was heavy.

c) He worked hard. – He didn't succeed.

d) … his intelligence. – He failed the exam.

Aufgabe 11 Bad times for crocodiles: Complete the sentences with the expressions in brackets.

Crocodiles are disappearing rapidly from the earth. It is estimated that hundreds of crocodiles are shot at night. (Grund) _____ hunters kill these animals is their skin. (Je … desto …) _____ their skins are in demand for making bags, shoes and so on, _____ crocodiles lose their lives. (Trotz) _____ strict laws forbidding the killing of these animals, the slaughtering goes on. (Trotz) _____ severe punishment by the State of Nigeria, the reptiles will be gone in a few years. The places where crocodiles can live become fewer. Swamps are often drained (Absicht) _____ win new land for growing vegetables for Europe. It seems that (Vergleich) _____ animal is _____ in danger of dying out _____ the crocodile.

... rund um den Satz: Sprechabsichten 129

Aufgabe 12   Why did the dinosaurs die out? Complete the sentences using appropriate expressions.

One theory is the following: _____ the dinosaurs died out is that they had no covering such as hair or feathers. Birds and mammals need these coverings _____ to keep warm in cold weather. _____ the dinosaurs were warm-blooded, they could only live in a warm climate. When the earth temperatures fell at the beginning of one of the ice ages, no animal was _____ in danger of dying out. The _____ the climate became, the _____ dinosaurs perished. Finally they became extinct.

Aufgabe 13   Compound nouns. Combine the words in capital letters with each word of the list below.

HOUSE	DAY	SIDE	LAND	MASTER
light	break	river	slide	head
work	pay	bed	father	piece
hen	time	walk	mark	stroke
warming	light	line	lord	school

Aufgabe 14   Spelling: Fill in the correct letter.

c	or	z	a high pri__e, win the first pri__e
i	or	ai	The sun r__ses. The gentleman r__sed his hat.
que	or	c	publi__, anti__
ea	or	e	wh__ther, w__ther
h	or	wh	a __ole in my sock, on the __ole
e	or	a	a correspond__nt, a shop assist__nt
y	or	i	happ__ly, sh__ly
x	or	xc	e__ellent, e__ept, e__amine, e__iting, e__ert
ei	or	ie	y__ld, c__ling
s	or	c	de__ease, di__ease

12 Textproduktion

12.1 Briefe

Die äußere Form von Briefen

Hier siehst du ein Beispiel für einen Standardbrief. Achte besonders auf folgende Punkte:
- Wo stehen im Brief welche Informationen?
- An welchen Stellen wird welche Zeichensetzung gebraucht?
- Wann wird im Brief groß- und wann kleingeschrieben?
- Bei formellen Briefen muss im Briefkopf immer der Adressat angegeben sein. Bei persönlichen Briefen entfällt dies.

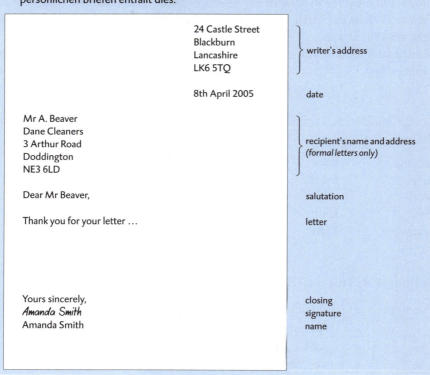

Die einzelnen Teile des Briefes
- **Absender** *(sender's address)*: Die Adresse des Absenders kann mit oder ohne Satzzeichen geschrieben werden, auf jeden Fall musst du dich für eine Variante entscheiden.
- **Datum** *(date):* Den Monat solltest du ausschreiben. Im amerikanischen Englisch schreibt man zuerst den Monat, dann den Tag und dann das Jahr: March 6th, 2004.
- **Absender und Datum** *(sender's address and date):* Notiere sie am rechten Briefrand untereinander.
- **Empfängername und -adresse** *(recipient's name and address):* Bei formellen Briefen schreibst du den Namen und die Adresse des Empfängers auf den linken Briefrand.
- **Anrede** *(salutation)*
- **Brief** *(letter)*
- **Schluss** *(closing)*
- **Unterschrift** *(signature)*
- **Name** *(name)*

Anrede und Briefschluss
- Wenn du den Namen des Empfängers nicht kennst:
  Verwende bei einem männlichen Empfänger 'Sir', bei einem weiblichen Empfänger 'Madam'. Wenn du dir nicht sicher bist, verwende 'Sir or Madam'.
  Beispiele:
Anrede (*salutation*)	Schluss (*closing*)
Dear Sir	
Dear Madam	Yours faithfully
Dear Sir or Madam	

- Wenn du den Namen des Empfängers kennst:
  Bei einer verheirateten Frau verwendest du '*Mrs*', bei einer unverheirateten '*Miss*'. Wenn du es nicht weißt, verwendest du '*Ms*'.
  Beispiele:
Anrede (*salutation*)	Schluss (*closing*)
Dear Mr James	
Dear Mrs Roberts	Yours sincerely
Dear Miss Berry	
Dear Ms Bell	

- Wenn du jemanden gut kennst und ihn mit Vornamen anredest:
  Beispiele:
Anrede (*salutation*)	Schluss (*closing*)
Dear Jane	Best wishes
Dear Mike	Love (nur bei sehr guten Freunden und nicht zwischen Männern)

Aufgabe 1   A request for tourist information

You intend to go to Edinburgh for a holiday. Write a letter to the Tourist Information Office and ask for brochures, price lists for accommodation (bed and breakfasts, hotels, campsites, bungalows, caravans). Ask for a map of the area and leaflets about holiday activities. Write a polite ending.

Aufgabe 2   Birthday

a) A birthday invitation: Invite your friend to your birthday. Give date, time and ask him/her to bring something to eat and drink. Fine weather? Party in the garden?

b) Accept the invitation. You will bring ...

c) ou can't accept the invitation. Give a reason.

Aufgabe 3   A hotel reservation

Write a letter to a hotel and reserve __ rooms. Give arrival and departure dates. Give type of rooms. Vegetarian meals? Write a polite ending.

Aufgabe 4   Postcards

a) Write a postcard to your friend from a holiday in Spain. Write about the weather, people, and a new friend. What's he/she like? Where's the hotel situated? Your activities and night life. Greetings to friends ...

b) Write a postcard to your friend about your skiing holiday in Austria. Write about the weather and your skiing skills.

12.2 E-Mails

E-Mails sind normalerweise **weniger förmlich als Briefe**.
- **Persönliche E-Mails** sind wie geschriebene Unterhaltungen. Sie enthalten Kurzformen, leichte Grammatik, Füllwörter, Verallgemeinerungen, persönliche Meinungen …
- **Formelle E-Mails** sollten dem Stil formeller Briefe folgen.
- Du solltest den Inhalt formeller E-Mails so kurz und präzise wie möglich halten.
- Du solltest auf E-Mails in dem Stil antworten, in dem die Person an dich geschrieben hat.

    Beispiele: Dear Ms Smith – Best wishes, John Dunn
    Dear Mr Dunn – Best wishes, Mandy Smith
    Dear Mike – Jane
    Dear Jane – Mike
- Da E-Mails gewöhnlich weniger förmlich sind als Briefe, sind *Best wishes* oder *Kind regards* passendere Schlussformeln. Persönliche E-Mails können auch nur mit dem Namen schließen. (Beachte: Viele E-Mails haben heute weder Anrede noch Schluss.)
- Gib immer einen passenden Betreff an, damit der Empfänger weiß, worum es in deiner E-Mail geht.

Aufgabe 5 Lost property in a hotel
Write an e-mail to the hotel in which you spent your holidays asking them to send your films which you forgot in your room. Give date and room number. Explain why the films are important for you.

Aufgabe 6 Complaint
Write an e-mail to a music shop in England with the following complaint: You were in England and ordered CDs in a music shop; you paid by cheque; they promised you to send the CDs soon. The cheque was cashed, but the CDs haven't arrived yet. Ask for information.

Aufgabe 7 Recommending a good book (e-mail)
Recommend a book to your friend. What is the book about? Why do you like it?

Aufgabe 8 A thank-you e-mail
Friends of yours in Britain sent you articles about the BBC. You must give a talk on the BBC in your class. The articles are very helpful. Write a thank-you e-mail to your friends.

Aufgabe 9 Excuse for not writing
Write an e-mail to your friend. You didn't write for a long time because you had exams and you were ill. You promise you'll e-mail more often.

Aufgabe 10 Cinema
a) Write an e-mail to your friend asking him/her to go to the cinema with you. Give film suggestions, time and date. Suggest doing something after the film.
b) Write a short text message telling your friend that you would like to see a comedy.

12.3 *Summary*

Das *summary* ist die Zusammenfassung eines Textes. Seine Länge beträgt in etwa 25 bis 30 % der Länge des Ausgangstextes. Das *summary* eines Textes von 500 Wörtern umfasst also 125 bis 150 Wörter. Das bedeutet, dass nur die wichtigsten Inhalte des Ausgangstextes im *summary* wiedergegeben werden. Das *summary* muss aber trotzdem so aussagekräftig sein, dass es einer Person, die den Ausgangstext nicht kennt, eine klare Vorstellung des Textinhalts vermittelt.

Wie fasst man zusammen?
- Folge dem Gedankengang des Textes.
- Begnüge dich mit den Fakten, füge keine eigenen Gedanken oder Interpretationen hinzu.
- Vermeide Wiederholungen, auch wenn sie im Text vorkommen sollten.
- Wandle direkte Rede in indirekte Rede um.
- *I* wird zu *he/she* (3. Person).
- Verwende das Präsens, um Texte zusammenzufassen.
- Verkürze jeden Abschnitt auf 25 bis 30 %.
- Verwende deine eigenen Worte, soweit dies möglich ist.

Tipps

- Lies den Text zunächst mehrmals, damit du ihn vollständig verstehst.
- Unterstreiche die wichtigsten Punkte.
- Schlage unbekannte Wörter nach.
- Versuche, den Text mithilfe von kurzen Ausdrücken zu straffen.
- Arbeite den Text Absatz für Absatz durch.
- Wenn die Länge des *summary* in der Aufgabenstellung vorgegeben ist, dann halte dich unbedingt an diese Wortzahl.
- Lies dein *summary* und frage dich: Ist es kurz und prägnant? Kann jemand, der den Text nicht gelesen hat, anhand meines *summary* das Wesentliche verstehen? Habe ich den Text mit meinen eigenen Worten wiedergegeben?

Aufgabe 11 Read the text carefully.

Maximillian Forsyth-Brown. How he hated that name. He'd endured it all his life so far: all sixteen years of it. How could anyone seriously say the name Maximillian Forsyth-Brown without raising their head slightly, putting their nose in the air and spluttering out the words like a dying carp struggling for air? Just then the doorbell rang. "Hi, is Max in?"

"I'll just get him for you, James," said Mrs Forsyth-Brown as she looked disapprovingly at the young boy dirtying her front doorstep before turning around to call Max.

"Maximillian, it's James for you."

How he hated that tone his mother put on. Why couldn't she be like everyone else and just say Max? Max! Not Maximillian, who sounded like a little soft kid from the posh end of town – and why couldn't she ever use his friends' proper names: Jim, Pete, Jas, not James, Peter and Jaswander?

a) Connect the following words and expressions with their meanings.

1 (to) endure   A upper-class area
2 (to) frown at   B something that one has had to live with that one does not like at all
3 (to) put on
4 (to) splutter   C (here) gentle, almost weak / not tough
5 posh end   D speak with difficulty
6 soft   E to show your dislike by the face you make
   F (here) used / adopted

1	2	3	4	5	6

b) Summarise the text in about 60 words.

Aufgabe 12   Write a summary of the following text:

Recent estimates tell us that about 100 million people make use of the international network of computers. Experts are of the opinion that this medium will soon change the way we communicate, shop, study and conduct business. The Internet has unlimited possibilities. In an hour's time the users of the Net can send messages to people all over the world, buy goods order holiday vacations and read a particular newspaper article without buying the newspaper.

Another way of using the Internet is sending Emails. If you have access to the Internet you can send a message to most parts of the world provided that the addressee has also access to the Internet.

This way of communicating is very fast and does usually not cost more than a local telephone call. E-mail are undoubtedly the most important means of communicating since the American Alexander Graham Bell invented telephone.

Lösungen

1 Präpositionen

Aufgabe 1 at, on, in, on, on, in, in, on, in, in, on, at, on, at, on, at, in, on, at/on

Aufgabe 2 at, for, against, at, towards, against, at, for, to, to/at, towards, at

Aufgabe 3 in the opinion, by heart, on his own, in bed, in tears, in paint, in common, in love, In turn, By chance, in sight, Out of sight, out of place, in fact, by far, out of sight, in public, In private, on holiday, by car, by plane/by air, By the way

Aufgabe 4 in, at, to, on, to, on, of, of, to, at, of, of, of, of, of

Aufgabe 5 to, at, to, at, at, at, to, to, to, to, to, to, to, at

Aufgabe 6
a) She gave me the form and asked me to fill it in.
b) Is this the purse you were looking for?
c) I like the people I work with.
d) Do you know who this music was composed by?
e) Do you know the girl Tom is talking to?
f) That's the type of book my father would be interested in.
g) He's the boy I told you about.
h) When was she operated on?
i) I've got lots of CDs I never listen to.
j) Yesterday I met a friend I went to school with.

Lösungen: Präpositionen

k) It's an invitation to a party I've been invited to.
l) What are you worried about?

Aufgabe 7 At, since, in, at, in, for, in, on, at, from, until (till), By, in, on

Aufgabe 8
a) at the same time
b) at present
c) At first
d) at last
e) At the same time
f) at last
g) At times
h) At first
i) for the time being/at present
j) at last
k) At times
l) at present

Aufgabe 9
a) on time
b) in time
c) behind the times
d) Once upon a time
e) in times of
f) for the time being

Aufgabe 10 While, Before, until, After, after, Before, During, until, During, while, before, until, during, after

Aufgabe 11
a) **Downtown** means business centre of a town or city
b) To **download** is to move information or programs to a computer
c) A **downer** is a drug that makes a person's mind and body less active
d) He goes **down under** means he goes to Australia or New Zealand

Aufgabe 12
a) write, playwright, rite, Right, arms, arms, alms
b) disease [diˈziːz], decease [diˈsiːs]; seize [siːz], cease [siːs]

2 Adjektive

Aufgabe 1 sick, poor, rich, brave, courageous, injured, curious/thirsty

Aufgabe 2 ill, frightened, sick, sleepy, well, Healthy, afraid

Aufgabe 3
a) biggest/largest
b) healthier
c) most astonishing
d) busier, more stressed
e) most important
f) more hopeful
g) luckier
h) more satisfied
i) cleverest
j) richest

Aufgabe 4 During World War II, there was not enough sugar in the US or in Europe, so the governments rationed it, i.e. people could not have as much as they wanted. The worst rationings were those of sugar and petrol. Americans and Europeans had to do with less sugar, which meant fewer lumps of sugar or teaspoons of sugar in the coffee or tea. The Coca Cola Company was in a bad situation which became worse when Cuba limited her sugar exports to the US. Coca Cola directors managed to convince the US government that Coke was important for the morale of the troops fighting abroad and therefore the company had the least rationing of sugar.

Aufgabe 5
a) nearest, next
b) latest, last
c) latter
d) little, less, least
e) farther, farthest
f) older, elder
g) bad, worse, worst

Aufgabe 6 most popular, Less, most secret, less, most famous, further, further, less, less

Aufgabe 7
a) length, breadth, depth, height, width
b) Estonian, Lithuanian, Latvian, Czech, Slovene, Slovak, Hungarian, Cypriot, Maltese, Polish

Lösungen: Adverbien

Aufgabe 8
a) ex-President
b) car-crash
c) three-hundred-ton ship
d) hand-made
e) doggie-bag
f) credit card

3 Adverbien

Aufgabe 1
a) drastically
b) Actually, economically
c) highly, historically, busy
d) Due, dull
e) mostly, irresistibly, nearly
f) increasingly, due, typically, high, heartily, gentle
g) economic, fantastically
h) Lately
i) mainly, high, absolutely
j) wholly
k) most, Lately, publicly, great, hardly, serious, desperately

Aufgabe 2 best-known, intensively, densely, essentially, highly, mostly, largely, sufficient, considerable, busy, weekly, richly, beautifully

Aufgabe 3
a) late, lately
b) well, well, good
c) hard, hardly, hard, hardly
d) nearly, near, nearly, nearly
e) free, freely, freely

Aufgabe 4
a) good, excellent, finely, particularly, wonderful
b) good, well, really, soft, incredibly, well, prettiest

Aufgabe 5
a) You mustn't always forget to put the milk in the fridge, it could turn sour.
b) Don't behave in such a silly way.

Lösungen: Adverbien | 141

c) Don't look at me so angrily.
d) Look more carefully to the left and right before you cross the street.
e) The music in your room sounds terribly loud.
f) Your socks smell bad.
g) You sound so silly.
h) Don't get furious if the meal doesn't taste good.
i) You look so untidy in your torn jeans.
j) After all, I'd like to get on well with you.

Aufgabe 6
a) Phil has recently emigrated with his parents from Pakistan.
b) He has been living in Manchester for two months now.
c) He speaks English well, but at home he often speaks Pakistani with his parents.
d) He often goes with them to the cinema at the weekends.
e) He arrived only a fortnight ago, and he can hardly speak English.
f) Kim is particularly interested in Kung Fu films. Since his arrival he has been to the cinema twice to see his favourite films.
g) Kim's parents could hardly find a flat in Manchester. Kim's father complains that white British people find a flat more easily.
h) Oddly enough, though they come from completely different parts of the world, Phil and Kim are British subjects, too.
i) Deeply-rooted prejudice against other races has often been (severely) criticized severely in Britain. Undoubtedly Britain is still far from being a multi-racial society.

Aufgabe 7
a) The cowboys believe optimistically that good will always triumph over evil.
b) He never treats strangers in an unfriendly way.
c) He works hard, he does his job tenaciously, he is always happy.
d) The cowboy became well-known in America immediately after the Civil War when cattle were needed urgently in the rapidly growing towns in the northern states.

e) In the 1890s the situation changed radically with the coming of the railroads and he was no longer used to drive cattle to the North.
f) Originally the cowboy was simply a farm labourer on horseback.
g) The modern cowboy uses pickup trucks daily and occasionally helicopters to manage cattle all over the West.
h) There were relatively few cowboys, probably not more than 50,000 in the United States during the cattle boom.
i) Nowadays it is hardly known that nearly two thirds of the cowboys were Blacks or Mexicans.
j) In the cowboy myth, the cowboy is always white and frequently a southerner. He seldom herds cattle, he mainly rescues innocent girls and he fights bandits courageously.

Aufgabe 8
a) All together
b) altogether
c) all-in
d) all-rounder

4 Zeitformen des Verbs

Aufgabe 1
a) comes
b) are, will visit
c) opens
d) won't lend, gives
e) leaves
f) I am
g) arrives
h) has
i) work

Aufgabe 2
a) Do you know, is typing, is cleaning
b) is listening
c) works, is working
d) leaves
e) see, are becoming
f) do not go, go, enjoy
g) are waiting, know
h) wants

Lösungen: Zeitformen des Verbs | 143

    i) look forward, am looking forward
    j) smokes, is preparing
    k) do not run, are running
    l) speaks, is learning
    m) is talking, seems
    n) like, smells
    o) hate
    p) do you prefer
    q) is seeing
    r) go
    s) is smelling, doesn't know
    t) are coming, is tasting
    u) is playing, suppose
    v) do you think, consider
    w) wish
    x) are looking, suits
    y) belongs

Aufgabe 3
    a) tastes, is tasting
    b) is smelling, smells

Aufgabe 4 wonder, know, come, is waiting, stopping, lives, come, are visiting, is getting into, rushes off, are you driving, drive, drive, is arriving, are driving, are shouting, Do you like, feel, are having, fetch, drink, do not want, spend, go, ends, hope, like, think

Aufgabe 5
    a) wanted, were sleeping, did
    b) was looking, saw, was missing
    c) was having, was making/made
    d) began, were driving
    e) was, was buzzing, managed

f) was studying
g) were wearing, suited
h) looked, was screaming
i) returned, was working
j) were sleeping/slept, woke
k) were flying, began
l) was walking, jumped, tore
m) was walking, blew
n) was shining
o) was writing
p) broke, he was roller blading
q) was setting
r) was working, broke

Aufgabe 6
a) ... were having breakfast when the postman rang.
b) ... were lying on the beach in the sun ...
c) ... was playing a computer game from two to four.
d) ... was phoning, ... stole her purse from her bag.

Aufgabe 7 existed, took, loved, made, showed, were playing, changed, went, could not believe, was waiting, was, were wearing, were, were screaming, began, was listening to, did not understand, were making, did not leave, were waiting, disappointed, learned, were playing, were selling

Aufgabe 8
a) Have you had breakfast yet? / Have you already had breakfast?
b) Have you ever flown before?
c) Have you ever been to Munich?
d) Have you already read the Munich guide?
e) Have you brought your inline skates?

Lösungen: Zeitformen des Verbs | 145

Aufgabe 9 since, for, since, for, Since

Aufgabe 10
a) has not been, since
b) has not rained for, have not had, for
c) have eaten, since
d) has advised, since, since, has risen
e) have not had, since

Aufgabe 11
a) has locked
b) have never seen
c) have been living here
d) have been looking
e) have been waiting
f) have known
g) has been sitting
h) have been playing
i) haven't heard
j) have been ringing
k) has been studying
l) have always hated
m) have you been learning
n) has knocked
o) have been relaxing

Aufgabe 12 has been eating, have been working, Have you been playing, have been lying, Have you been playing

Aufgabe 13 has continued, issued, has licensed, has been, have been analyzing, have not found, have Stan and Ollie remained, have seen, have been laughing, has been attracting

Aufgabe 14
a) arrived
b) had not expected, said
c) had been able, took
d) had even had, left
e) gave, was, was

Lösungen: Zeitformen des Verbs

Aufgabe 15 was, was, ran, often watched, had already learned, had already written, was not, began, had acted, came, was, had already toured, liked, had learned, failed, changed, came, had played, had founded, engaged, meant

Aufgabe 16 were, had never dreamt, had left, had been working, was, had been recording, had started, had been rising, had been taking

Aufgabe 17
a) am going to buy, will buy
b) is going to rain, will get wet
c) am not going to lend

Aufgabe 18
a) This year I'm going to spend my holidays in Cornwall.
b) I'm going to book my crossing from Cherbourg to Weymouth soon.
c) I'm going to visit Land's End and some old tin mines.
d) Will there be many tourists?
e) Will there be any vacancies in bed and breakfast places?
f) Do you think it will rain a lot in August?

Aufgabe 19
a) Petra: This time next week I'll be walking on top of the cliffs.
b) Jens: I'll be visiting Celtic stone circles.
c) Georg: I'll be drinking/having a beer in the "Jamaica Inn".
d) Babsi: I'll be surfing all day long.
e) Michael: I'll be making an excursion to the Scilly Isles.

Aufgabe 20
a) Petra: At the end of my holidays I'll have hiked/walked on/climbed up dozens of cliffs.
b) Jens: I'll have taken lots of photos of Celtic sacrificial sites.
c) Georg: I'll have had/drunk a beer in a typically Cornish pub.
d) Babsi: I'll have learned how to surf in the Atlantic Ocean.
e) Michael: I'll have visited the Tropical Museum on the Scilly Isles.

Lösungen: Passiv 147

Aufgabe 21 is, presented, will be, opened, have seen, have appeared, opened, had translated, can see, owns, have been trying, "I will not allow", is running

Aufgabe 22 has, have been using up, are growing, kill/are killing, it will not be, cut down, will be destroyed, keep, is dying, Will all forests have disappeared?, are going to live, have been ruining, is

Aufgabe 23 disappear, distrust, unload, discontinue, undo, disagree, unlock, unplug, disapprove, disobey

5 Passiv

Aufgabe 1 a) is weighed, is announced, hand luggage is controlled, is given, his seat on the plane is shown to him
b) be weighed, will be announced, hand luggage will be controlled, will be given to him, seat on the plane will be shown to him
c) was weighed, was announced, hand luggage was controlled, was given to him, seat on the plane was shown to him
d) have been weighed, will have been announced, hand luggage will have been controlled, will have been given to him, seat on the plane will have been shown to him
e) been weighed, had been announced, hand luggage had been controlled, had been given to him, seat on the plane had been shown to him

Aufgabe 2 a) Der Safe war sorgfältig verschlossen worden.
b) Vergangene Nacht wurde er von Einbrechern aufgebrochen.
c) Das ganze Geld wurde gestohlen.
d) Bis jetzt sind keine Fingerabdrücke entdeckt worden.
e) Werden die Einbrecher je gefangen werden?
f) Die Einbrecher würden gefasst werden, wenn Sherlock Holmes den Fall übernähme.

Lösungen: Passiv

g) Der Safe wäre nicht aufgebrochen worden, wenn das Alarmsystem funktioniert hätte.

h) Schließlich wurden die Einbrecher festgenommen, weil der Fall Inspektor Columbo übergeben worden war.

Aufgabe 3

a) Many parents are said to have too little time for their children.

b) Quite a lot of fathers are said to spend more time watching football on TV than talking to their children.

c) Children are known to need their parent's time and love.

d) Mothers are often criticized for taking up employment instead of caring for their families.

e) Single parents are often wrongly considered to be incapable of raising children.

f) The state is expected to compensate for the lack of attention to children by ...

Aufgabe 4

a) The Indians were defeated (by the Whites).

b) They were almost wiped out.

c) Their land was taken away.

d) All the treaties with the Indians had been broken.

e) They had been driven into areas with infertile soil.

f) These areas were called reservations.

g) The Indians were said to be an inferior race.

h) The Indians were known as .../to be brave fighters.

i) The Native Americans are helped today.

j) They will be given land with fertile soil.

k) Better education has been organized for them.

l) Their health is cared for.

m) They are often helped to build up a tourist industry.

n) They have been given civil rights. – Civil rights have been given to them.

Lösungen: Passiv

Aufgabe 5
a) The coloured people were not given the right to vote.
The right to vote was not given to the coloured people.
b) They were paid low wages.
Low wages were paid to them.
c) They were constantly shown their inferiority.
Their inferiority was constantly shown to them.
d) The blacks were denied equal job opportunities.
Equal job opportunities were denied to the blacks.
e) The underprivileged were given shabby houseing in the homelands.
Shabby houseing in the Homelands was given to them.
f) The coloured population was promised improvements that were never realized.
Improvements that were never realized were promised to the coloured population.
g) The blacks were taught absolute obedience.
Absolute obedience was taught to the blacks.
h) In the end, Nelson Mandela, who broke the whites' power, had to be given freedom.
In the end, freedom had to be given to Nelson Mandela, who broke the whites' power.

Aufgabe 6
a) Our pets were looked after by our neighbour.
b) The key was looked for everywhere.
c) This matter must be looked into more carefully.
d) These words can be looked up in a dictionary.
e) The radio was switched on.
f) The house had been broken into.
g) A specialist will be called for.
h) What is this tool used for?
i) The match was called off because of the rain.
j) The dishes were put away 10 minutes ago.

Aufgabe 7
a) has been overfished
b) are being threatened

Lösungen: Modale Hilfsverben

      c) is caught, is sold
      d) have been motivated
      e) are being ordered, are considered
      f) can be saved
      g) has not been supported
      h) can be made / earned
      i) can be seen, has been taken, are being caught
      j) must be given
      k) are rewarded, can be used

Aufgabe 8
      a) She is known ...
      b) ... she had been trained as a nurse and a midwife.
      c) She was imprisoned ...
      d) After the American birth control league had been founded ...
      e) ... sex education was ...
      f) ... were informed, ... about family planning.
      g) ... her social work for women was adopted ...

Aufgabe 9 snow-covered, hand-knitted, long-haired, well-dressed, well-meant, self-centred, self-controlled, self-employed

Aufgabe 10 repeating, omitting, differed, preferred, fulfilled, permitted, cancelled

6 Modale Hilfsverben

Aufgabe 1 haven't been able, can, couldn't, can't, have been able, couldn't, couldn't, was able, couldn't, were able, could, can, can't, can't, can, couldn't, were able, could, could, were able, will be able

Aufgabe 2
      a) can/could, can, could, can, will be able to
      b) Can, can't, can

Lösungen: Modale Hilfsverben | 151

c) couldn't, can/could
d) Were you able to, would have been able to
e) could, can
f) could, can, have been able to, can/are able to, can/are able
g) can't, Can/Could, could have

Aufgabe 3
a) I may/might spend my next holiday in Ireland.
b) May I use the/your phone?
c) May I try your new Mountain Bike?
d) Be careful! The path may/might be icy/slippery.
e) I haven't invited him, but I might have invited him if I'd known him better.
f) I may/might be home later from school because I want to go to town with a friend.
g) She may/might have gone shopping.
h) Please don't phone me this evening because I might/may be learning English vocabulary as we may/might have a test tomorrow.

Aufgabe 4
a) Will/Would you bring me the bill, please?
b) Would you like another piece of cake?
c) Would you like to go to the cinema with me this evening?
d) Will you listen?
e) Sorry I'm late but my car wouldn't start.
f) My father would read me a story every evening.
g) Will/would you help me with my homework?
h) Would you like me to bring you an aspirin?/I'll bring you an aspirin. You'll feel better soon.
i) Will you shut the living-room door?
j) I've missed the bus. Will/would you drive me to school?

Lösungen: Modale Hilfsverben

Aufgabe 5
a) You should have come to the party. It was great!
b) You look tired. You should go to bed.
c) I feel sick. I shouldn't have eaten so much.
d) Smoking shouldn't be allowed in restaurants.
e) I think Margaret should pass her driving test.
f) Shall I carry your bags? They look very heavy.
g) Shall we have a game of tennis on Saturday?
h) Shall I buy the blue jeans or the black ones?
i) These chocolate biscuits are delicious. You should try one.
j) You should have your hair cut before your interview.
k) Shall I gift-wrap it?

Aufgabe 6 must, needn't/won't have to, must/will have to, have to, must, will have to, mustn't, needn't/won't have to, mustn't, mustn't, must, must

Aufgabe 7
a) could, can, must, must, may
b) couldn't/wasn't able to, had to, can/could/will/would, must
c) had to, couldn't have, Can/Could/Would

Aufgabe 8 should have given up, could take over, will/should become, would like, can walk, can't/aren't able to go, must/have to be, must/have to take part, can't/aren't able to go, can, couldn't/wasn't able to do, may be, have to enroll, must/has to be, should have, should find, should be, should be

Aufgabe 9 breathtaking, far-reaching, good-looking, easy-going

Aufgabe 10 named, nameless, praiseworthy, praising, hopeful, believable, replacing, courageous, noiseless, gracious

7 Gerundium

Aufgabe 1
a) of watching
b) of drawing, acting
c) for moving, in writing
d) of delivering
e) of being killed
f) for starting
g) of founding
h) by creating
i) of earning
j) of working

Aufgabe 2
a) on making
b) in becoming
c) on inventing
d) of drawing, with making
e) of giving
f) on having
g) in making
h) of building
i) from watching
j) of taking

Aufgabe 3
a) of opening
b) about visiting
c) at building
d) about going
e) about watching
f) of watching
g) on building
h) for imitating
i) for having
j) at being able, at being allowed

Aufgabe 4
a) He aims at showing that revolutions are always followed by tyranny.
b) The farmer, Mr Jones, is accustomed to treating the animals badly.
c) The animals dream of being free.
d) They are keen on driving out their human master, Mr Jones.
e) Mr Jones escapes by running away.
f) The animals agree with choosing two boars, Napoleon and Snowball, as their leaders.
g) Napoleon and Snowball are proud of being clever.
h) The animals are glad about living in peace.
i) Napoleon is interested in being the master of the farm.
j) The dogs forming Napoleon's bodyguard help him by driving Snowball away.

Lösungen: Gerundium

k) The pigs try to be like their former master by beginning to walk on their hind legs.
l) Napoleon succeeds in forming an alliance with nearby human farmers.
m) The animals are afraid of protesting.
n) Napoleon prevents the animals from living in freedom.
o) He oppresses the animals by saying: "All animals are equal, but some are more equal than others."

Aufgabe 5 had considered emigrating, for a long time, John couldn't stand working, any longer, give up/stop typing, suggested going, could not help discussing, could not delay making, did not risk being, did not delay following, suggested settling down, admits feeling, appreciate living, don't mind having, enjoy swimming and surfing very much, admits going, does not deny having

Aufgabe 6
a) helping other people
b) having made mistakes
c) working at the weekend
d) being helped by colleagues
e) working in a team
f) doing your work/job
g) making decisions
h) going abroad for your company
i) learning something new
j) working together with people
k) contradicting your boss
l) learning a difficult language for your job

Aufgabe 7
a) it's hard
b) It's no use/It's useless
c) It's worth
d) It must be great
e) a pleasure/fun
f) no denying the fact
g) It's worth
h) It's no use/It's useless

Aufgabe 8
a) … is used to/accustomed to living in the Indian jungle together with wolves.
b) … think of sending him back to civilization.
c) … is angry at having to leave his friends.
d) It is no use/no good staying …

e) ... has a lot of problems accompanying him ...
f) Mowgli succeeds in defeating the tiger.
g) ... Mowgli is delighted about meeting Kitty, the daughter of an English major.
h) ... he doesn't mind returning to civilization
i) ... had difficulty in imitating the movements of the many different animals
j) ... is worth seeing/watching.

8 Infinitiv

Aufgabe 1
a) made
b) let
c) let
d) make
e) let
f) let
g) let's

Aufgabe 2 let, let, made, let, let, made, let

Aufgabe 3 Why not go, would rather not go, had better, had better not, would rather

Aufgabe 4
a) climb, go, open
b) ring up
c) escaping
d) arrive
e) searching
f) say

Aufgabe 5
I plan to go to England.
I'd like to visit Stonehenge.
I wish to meet Prince Charles.
I intend to hire a pony in Wales.
I expect the sun to shine all the time.
I hope to find new friends there.
I prefer to stay overnight in my tent.

Lösungen: Infinitiv

Aufgabe 6 advised me to check, recommended to me not to take, told me to tie, asked me to take a photograph, allowed me to change/swap, told us to fasten, forced one of the passengers to open, I was allowed to leave

Aufgabe 7
a) I should be delighted to help you,
b) I'm glad to see that now you are no longer depressed.
c) They will be very surprised to hear this news.
d) We were shocked to hear of the accident.
e) Daisy was worried to see that her boyfriend was ill.
f) Of course Peter was very pleased to find a new job.
g) Kevin's parents were sad to hear that he had failed his exam.
h) We were sorry to see that a car had injured the dog.
i) Carol was happy to find out that she hadn't lost her car key.
j) I'm sorry to have to tell you that you didn't win the race.

Aufgabe 8
a) It would be foolish to believe his promise.
b) It is dangerous to cross the street during the rush-hour.
c) It is wrong to judge people by their appearance.
d) It is crazy to go out in this terrible weather.
e) It was strange to see his behaviour.
f) It is difficult to learn a foreign language without any help.
g) It is clever to compare prices in different shops before buying something.
h) It is disappointing to get bad marks in a test you worked hard for.
i) It is not as simple as it looks to learn inline-skating.
j) It is sad to see how nature is polluted.

Aufgabe 9 is likely to arrive at 8 p.m., is unlikely to go by car, is sure/certain to be

Aufgabe 10
a) If Carol had a friend to go out with, she would be happier.
b) She says she can't go to the dinner party without having anything to wear.

c) We'd like to have a house in the country to live closer to nature.
d) Haven't you got anything to open the bottle with?
e) This is a dentist to trust.
f) They bought a house to renovate.
g) I don't know anybody to take care of your dog when you are on holiday.
h) We need somebody to repair our computer.

Aufgabe 11
a) for Americans to pay
b) for teenage girls and boys to work
c) for Americans to shake
d) for Americans to keep
e) for many Americans to stay
f) For many of them, to learn
g) for foreigners to understand
h) for Americans to use
i) for Americans to plan
j) for Americans to celebrate

Aufgabe 12
a) There weren't enough finger prints for the police to detect the thief.
b) In some parts of American cities there is too much violence for the police to cope with.
c) Today there is too intensive cooperation between the police in European countries for terrorists to escape.
d) Many people say that our laws are not severe enough for criminals to be deterred.
e) In the US lie detectors are considered to be useful enough for the police to employ them more often.
f) Capital punishment of death by the electric chair is too cruel even for murderers to be killed by these means.
g) Hooliganism is too dangerous for society to make light of.
h) The fine is too high for the smuggler to pay.
i) The number of crimes is too high for the police to arrest all the law-breakers.

Aufgabe 13
a) They did not know where to settle down.
b) They did not know which corn to cultivate.

Lösungen: Infinitiv

c) They had no idea how to survive.
d) The asked the Indians how to use bows and arrows.
e) They wondered how to grow vegetables different from the English ones, such as pumpkins or potatoes.
f) They did not know how to build wooden houses without nails.
g) They were at a loss to know at what time of the year to plant seeds on the ground.
h) They had no idea how to fertilize their plants.
i) They asked the Indians where to find wild fruits and mushrooms.
j) When the Pilgrim Fathers had become successful farmers, they decided how to celebrate the first Thanksgiving.

Aufgabe 14
a) It was one of the most bitter experiences for the American nation to realize that the Soviet Union was the first to launch a satellite, the Sputnik, into orbit in 1957.
b) Yuri Gagarin was the first man to travel in space in 1961.
c) The first American to orbit the earth was John Glenn in 1962.
d) Apollo 11 was the only spaceship to land on the lunar Sea of Tranquility in 1969.
e) "Challenger" was the only space shuttle to explode in 1986.
f) The most expensive space programme to land on Mars was started in 1995.
g) Most people considered it (to be) absurd to land on Mars.
h) "Sojourner" was the first man-made object to land on Mars in 1997.
i) The most famous science fiction film to be seen on TV is Star Trek.

Aufgabe 15 to make, to use, to build up, to be, do, to find out, to predict, to run, to invent, to integrate, to compete, break, to let, become, influence

Aufgabe 16 to listen to, to conquer/conquering, to imitate, to make/making, to have, hearing, listening to

Lösungen: Infinitiv | 159

Aufgabe 17
a) having, to specialize
b) to working, to work, buying and selling
c) to buy, buying
d) switching
e) to watch, working
f) swimming, to swim
g) waiting
h) hearing
i) to send
j) to meeting, to see
k) to drink, to drinking, to give up, drinking

Aufgabe 18
Tennis: Wimbledon
a) In the 90s, Wimbledon spectators enjoyed watching fantastic tennis with German players.
b) Boris Becker and Steffi Graf made tennis world-famous by winning the World Championships repeatedly.
c) In 1985, seventeen-year-old Boris Becker was the youngest player to win Wimbledon.
d) In 1988, Steffi Graf succeeded in winning the women's title.

Soccer: The "Wembley Goal"
e) In 1966, the German fans denied losing the World Cup final in Wembley by saying that the third goal was not a goal.
f) The referee insisted on giving the goal good.
g) The German team refused to accept the referee's decision.
h) The English team was very lucky to win the World Cup.

Car racing
i) Michael Schumacher won the Formula I World Racing Championships in 1994 for the first time by relying on a car made by British engineers.
j) Today, instead of racing for British Benetton, Michael Schumacher races for the Italian Ferrari company.

Aufgabe 19 speech, growth, necessity, advertisement, preference, failure, seat, success, arrival, warning

Aufgabe 20 fasten, scissors, doubt, calm, ghost, reign, thumb

Aufgabe 21 steel, weak, pear, loose, waist, principle, flee, threw, site, knight

9 Indirekte Rede

Aufgabe 1
a) He said (that) he was a racing driver.
b) He said (that) he had been racing for just over a year.
c) He said (that) he had won a lot of races.
d) He said (that) he lived a dangerous life.
e) He said (that) he was going to buy a new Rolls Royce because he had crashed his old one.
f) He said (that) his next race would be in Monte Carlo.
g) He said (that) he would take me with him if I wanted.

Aufgabe 2
a) Because the advertisement said (that) their prices were very low.
b) Because my friend said (that) he knew the way.
c) Because his teacher had said (that) his mark was very good and (that) he'd /she'd (had) noticed a big improvement in his English.
d) Because she said/told him (that) her German teacher had given them so much homework that she would probably take all evening to finish it.
e) Because he said (that) his mountain bike had been stolen.
f) Because Ray said (that) he was ill in bed with a high temperature.
g) Because the neighbours said (that) they were vegetarians.
h) Because Frank said he would meet her in front of the cinema at 7.30.

Lösungen: Indirekte Rede 161

Aufgabe 3
a) He said (that) he felt great because his wife and son were going to join him the following/next day.
b) He said (that) he had arrived at Munich Airport three hours before.
c) He said (that) his first concert would be the following Saturday in Munich. The day before he had been in Hamburg. The fans had been great there.
d) He said (that) his wife and son would accompany him for the following/next two weeks.
e) He said (that) his son was doing fine. He had begun to walk two weeks before. They were looking forward to having another baby the following/next year and that they would like a girl.
f) He said (that) while they were in Germany they were going to buy a little old castle somewhere on top of a mountain. They needed a place where they could just relax and enjoy a normal family life.
g) He said (that) he really enjoyed being a father but he didn't see his son very often. The last time he had seen him was three weeks before, which was why he had brought his family to Germany.
h) He said (that) he was feeling fine. He'd had/He had had a bad cold the week before and had lost his voice but he was OK again. He would have to be careful that he didn't get too close to anyone. If he went down with another cold he would be forced to cancel the tour.
i) He said (that) they were going to do a sound check in the Olympia Concert Hall the next/following afternoon.
j) He said (that) it was fantastic to be in little old Germany again, and that he loved us all.

Aufgabe 4
a) He said (that) they believed that more people should be aware of how many plants and wild flowers were/are becoming rare or dying out.
b) He said (that) many flowers and plants which used to grow in the countryside in the 19th century were now unknown.
c) He said (that) we ought to do something soon because more and more species of wild animals would become extinct.
d) He said (that) the fines for dumping waste in rivers must/had to be so high that companies would no longer prefer to pay them instead of investing in recycling.
e) He said (that) if we didn't act now, it might be too late to save our planet.

Lösungen: Indirekte Rede

f) He said (that) we mustn't/weren't to shut our eyes to the misuse of the environment.
g) He said (that) the millions of dollars which governments spent on defence could be invested in protecting our environment.
h) He said (that) we had to put more pressure on the politicians.
i) He said (that) we should encourage our children to take care of the planet Earth.
j) He said (that) we couldn't go on polluting our environment and thinking we didn't have to/needn't worry about the consequences.

Aufgabe 5
a) He told us to put glass, tin and plastic into the special containers.
b) He suggested using our bikes or going on foot more often.
c) He invited us (to come) to an information evening the following/next Friday.
d) He offered to give us more information on recycling.
e) He asked us to set a good example by not leaving rubbish on the beach or in the countryside.
f) He told us not to use our cars so often.
g) He advised us to save energy by switching off unnecessary lights.
h) He offered us one of his booklets, 'Friends of the Earth'.
i) He asked us to join 'Friends of the Earth' or 'Greenpeace'.
j) He asked us to put some money in the box on our way out.
k) He invited us to join him for some organically-grown refreshments in the foyer.

Aufgabe 6
a) He asked me how old I was.
b) He wanted to know if/whether I'd had any experience of working with 10 to 11 year olds.
c) He enquired if/whether I thought I might have any problems speaking English all the time.
d) He asked me if/whether I spoke any other languages.
e) He wanted to know how long I could stay in the USA.

f) He enquired if/whether I had any friends or relatives in America.
g) He asked me if/whether there was any particular area of the USA that I would like to go to.
h) He wanted to know why I wanted to work in the USA.
i) He enquired if/whether that was the first time that I'd applied for a job like that.
j) He asked me if/whether I could imagine having problems with homesickness.
k) He wanted to know if/whether you would be prepared to give him your agreement in writing.
l) He enquired if/whether he should give me some more information about the sort of things I would be expected to do.
m) He asked me if/whether I was aware that once I'd signed the contract it would no longer be possible for me to change my mind.
n) He wanted to know if/whether I'd received the summer camp brochures they had sent me the week before.
o) He enquired if/whether I was be able to pay for the return flight to the USA myself.
p) He asked me what was the earliest date I could fly.
q) He wanted to know if/whether there was anything else I would like to ask him about the job.
r) He enquired whether/if I would mind giving him one or two days to consider my application before he let me know his decision.

Aufgabe 7
a) Jennifer asked Peter why he was so against television.
b) Peter said (that) he thought television was partly responsible for the break-up of family life.
c) Jennifer asked Peter how much time the average person spent watching television.
d) Peter answered (that) according to the latest statistics, between four in the afternoon and midnight, at least 12 million viewers were sure to be watching television. That figure could rise to 37 million at peak viewing hours.
e) Jennifer asked Peter if/whether he could suggest some things people could do instead of watching television.

f) Peter suggested going to the cinema or the theatre.
g) Jennifer wanted to know why so many people spent their evenings in front of the television.
h) Peter answered (that) the main reason had to be laziness. It was so easy to switch on the TV. Unfortunately, a lot of people just left it on even if they were not interested in the programme.
i) Jennifer told Peter (that) she was worried about the negative effect TV could have on her children. She asked Peter to give her some advice.
j) Peter advised her to choose the programmes her children watched very carefully. She should also sit with them while they were watching in case they had any questions.
k) Jennifer said (that) she often switched on the TV to relax after a long day at work. She asked Peter if/whether she should get rid of her television.
l) Peter told her (that) she didn't have to/needn't get rid of her television. He advised her to take up a sport or hobby which she could do in the evenings.
m) Jennifer wanted to know if there was anything else Peter/he would like to say.
n) Peter replied (that) there was more to life than sitting in front of a box. He warned us not to let television take over our lives.
o) Jennifer said that it had been very enjoyable talking to him. She invited him to join her for a coffee.
p) Peter said (that) he was sorry but he didn't have time for a coffee. He had to go home immediately because there was a programme on TV that he would like to watch. He suggested having a coffee together the next day.

Aufgabe 8 omit, commit, submit; receive, deceive, perceive, conceive

Aufgabe 9 Smiths', week's, children's, Jill's, James', boss', Alice's, John's, women's, ladies'

10 Relativsätze

Aufgabe 1
a) This man who has a British passport is a Pakistani.
b) This girl whose passport is blue is Indian.
c) Swansea, which is a trading centre, has racial minorities.

Aufgabe 2
a) The girl I met on the boat comes from Sri Lanka.
b) The gentleman you can see over there lives in Zimbabwe.
c) The jobs they want to have are not desirable.
d) These Asians waiting for permission to immigrate are from Burma.

Aufgabe 3
a) The problems we were talking about are serious.
b) The lady you are looking at works in an immigration office.
c) The waiter I always forget the name of comes from the West Indies.
d) The new law you have heard about restricts immigration.
e) The speech we listened to was about Kenya's independence.
f) The advantages they are entitled to are part of the welfare system.
g) This was the chance they were waiting for to immigrate.
h) The immigration figures Britain is faced with are high.

Aufgabe 4 which, of which, which, whose, who, which, whose, whose, whose, which

Aufgabe 5

Verb	Noun	Adjective
attract	attraction	attractive
fear	fear	fearful
vitalize	vitality	vital
originate	origin/originality	original
destroy	destruction	destructive
differ	difference	different
pride (oneself upon)	pride	proud
rely (on)	reliance	reliable

invent	invention	inventive
fascinate	fascination	fascinating

11 Sprechabsichten

Aufgabe 1 a) It was such a boring film that I nearly fell asleep.
The film was so boring that I nearly fell asleep.

b) It is such an expensive car that I can't buy it.
The car is so expensive that I can't buy it.

c) It is such a bad book that I can't read it.
The book is so bad that I can't read it.

Aufgabe 2 a) No (other) country exports more cars than Japan.

b) No car consumes more petrol than a Chevrolet.

c) No car is safer than a Volvo.

Aufgabe 3 a) The longer we stayed in London, the more we liked the city.

b) The less you eat, the less you weigh.

c) The more one practises, the better one plays an instrument.

Aufgabe 4 a) would find   b) want to buy
c) are interested in   d) would have seen
e) was/were fine   f) had saved

Aufgabe 5 were, would, would like, had, did not, could easily join, would you recommend, wanted, are, will lend

Aufgabe 6 a) If you don't open the door, I won't be able to come in.

b) If her eyes didn't ache, she wouldn't have to wear sunglasses.

c) If you don't remind me about Bill's birthday, I won't send him a birthday card.
d) If she didn't have a test tomorrow, she wouldn't feel terrible.
e) If Tom had revised for the test, he wouldn't have failed.
f) If his parents had given him the money, he would have been able to buy the interrail ticket.

Aufgabe 7
a) I'll work longer this week in order to have a day off tomorrow.
b) They spoke quietly in order not to wake the baby.
c) Read the text twice in order to understand it better.
d) He carried the vase carefully in order not to break it.

Aufgabe 8
a) Since/As he felt ill, Tom stayed in bed.
The reason why Tom stayed in bed was that he felt ill.
b) Since/As he was not qualified for the job, he did not get it.
The reason why he did not get the job was that he was not qualified for it.
c) Since/As the worker didn't work carefully, he was sacked.
The reason why the worker was sacked was that he did not work carefully.
d) Since/As her bag was very heavy, I carried it for her.
The reason why I carried her bag for her was that it was very heavy.

Aufgabe 9
a) in spite of
b) Although
c) Although
d) in spite of

Aufgabe 10
a) Although they don't have much money, they want to have a new car.
b) She walked quickly in spite of her heavy suitcase/although her suitcase was heavy.
c) Although he worked hard, he didn't succeed.
d) He failed the exam in spite of his intelligence.

Lösungen: Textproduktion

Aufgabe 11 The reason why, The more, the more, In spite of, In spite of, in order to, no animal is more, than

Aufgabe 12 the reason why, in order, Since/As, more, colder, more

Aufgabe 13 lighthouse, housework, henhouse, housewarming
daybreak, payday, daytime, daylight
riverside, bedside, sidewalk, sideline
landslide, fatherland, landmark, landlord
headmaster, masterpiece, masterstroke, schoolmaster

Aufgabe 14 price, prize; rises, raised; public, antique; whether, weather; hole, whole; correspondent, assistant; happily, shyly; excellent, except; examine, exciting, exert; yield, ceiling; decease, disease

12 Textproduktion

Aufgabe 1

Seeweg 7
64372 Oberramstadt
Germany
9th April 2005

The Tourist Information Office
15 Princess Street
Edinburgh
Scotland

Dear Sir or Madam,

A small group of us would like to spend a week in Edinburgh in the second week of August. As this will be our first visit to Scotland, we would be grateful if you could send us some information.
Firstly, would it be possible to send us some brochures including the price lists of hotels and bed and breakfast accommodation in and around Edinburgh. We would also like to know how much camping site accommodation is for tents, caravans or holiday bungalows. There will be four of us and we will be visiting

Edinburgh for a week from 7th August to the 14th August. Finally, could you send us some leaflets about holiday activities in Scotland, a city map of Edinburgh and if possible a map of the area around Edinburgh as we are interested in going on some walks in the countryside.
I look forward to hearing from you.

Yours faithfully

Philipp Hofmann

Philipp Hofmann

Aufgabe 2 a) Dear Andy,
Would you like to come to my birthday party on 3 August at 8 p.m? Could you bring a bottle or something to eat for the buffet? I really hope the weather will be fine so that we can have the party in the garden. Can you let me know as soon as possible if you can come or not?
Hope to see you on the 3th.
Love, Franziska

b) Dear Franziska,
Thanks for the invitation! I'd love to come to your party and I'll bring a dessert. I'm looking forward to seeing you on the 3rd.
Love
Sarah

c) Dear Franziska,
Thanks for the invitation to your party. I'm afraid I can't come because I'll be on holiday on the 3rd. Hope you have a great party.
Best wishes
Andy

Aufgabe 3 Dear Sir or Madam,
Your hotel has been recommended to me by a friend. I would like to reserve a double room with bath for my parents and a single room with shower for myself for 7 nights from the 1st September to the 7th September. If possible, we would like rooms with balconies and a view of the sea.
Could you please send me a price list of your rooms with half-board and enclose a brochure with a description of your hotel and its facilities.

As my mother is vegetarian, I would be grateful if you could inform me as to whether vegetarian meals are available at your hotel.
I look forward to receiving confirmation of my booking.
Kind regards
Luise Rotmeyer

Aufgabe 4

a) Dear Sandra,
I'm having a really great time here in Alicante. The weather's sunny and warm and the people are very friendly. I've made lots of friends here. One of them is English. His name's Pete and he's from Birmingham. He's tall with dark hair and blue eyes and he's very funny. He wants to become an actor when he leaves school. I think he would make a very good comedian! Anyway we're going to write to each other when the holiday is over. The beach is only 5 minutes away from the hotel and we go swimming every day. Yesterday I tried water skiing. It was great fun but I wasn't very good at it. It's difficult to keep your balance and I kept falling into the water.
The night life here is fantastic. Tomorrow evening we're all going to a disco together. I'm really looking forward to it.
How are things back home? When I see you next week I can tell you all about my holiday. Say hello to Jenny and Tina for me.
See you soon!
Love
Kelly

b) Dear Linda,
I'm staying with my parents near Salzburg in Austria. We're having a nice skiing holiday. The snow is good, the weather is sunny but cold. I've already got a good tan. My new skis are fantastic. I can go over bumps more easily and quickly. It's much more fun than last year with my old skis.
Love
Patty

Aufgabe 5

Reiter-Weg 12
10104 Berlin

Hotel Esplanade
Alicante
Spain

12. August 2004

Dear Sir or Madam,
When I returned from my holiday in Alicante I discovered that I had left three films in my hotel room. If these films have been found, I would be grateful if they could be sent to me as soon as possible to the address above.
I stayed in your hotel from 3 August – 10 August in room number 49. I think the films were in the top drawer of the bedside table.
I really hope that the films have been found as I had a wonderful holiday in Alicante and was looking forward to showing all my friends the photographs I took.
Thank you in advance.
Best regards
Birgit Schmidt

Aufgabe 6

Einstein-Allee 40
04347 Leipzig
Germany

World of Music Co
Brick Lane
Colchester
Essex CO11 HJ
England

7 October 2004

Dear Sir or Madam,
While I was in Colchester three weeks ago, I ordered two CDs of Irish Folk Music from your shop. The two CDs cost £30 and £5 for postage. I paid by cheque and was told that the CDs would be sent to me within a week. According to my bank statement the cheque to the amount of £35 has been cashed, but although three weeks have passed the CDs haven't arrived yet. Could you please look into the matter and find out what has happened.
I would be grateful if you could let me know when I can expect the CDs to arrive.

Thank you very much for your help and I look forward to hearing from you as soon as possible.

Yours faithfully

Frank Beyer

Aufgabe 7

Hi Kevin,
How are you? I've just finished reading a really good book and I wanted to tell you about it in this email. It's called *The Man Who Listens to Horses* by Monty Roberts. Have you seen the film with Robert Redford? The book is an autobiography and the author writes about how he learned to train horses without using cruelty or causing the animals pain which was the usual way to train horses in the USA at that time. He first tried out his special method when he was only seven years old and from then on the always managed to win the trust of horses. Of course, there is also romance in the book. The horse whisperer meets and falls in love with a woman whose daughter had a riding accident. He manages to win round the horse which is very wild and the girl gets over her fear of horses and riding. I don't want to tell you any more as it will spoil it for you when you read the book.
I really enjoyed the book because it is a true story and is well-written. I know you love animals and that horse-riding is one of your hobbies so I'm sure you'd like the book, too.
When you've read it, let me know what you thought of it.
All the best.
Daniel.

Aufgabe 8

Hauptstraße 22
82515 Wolfratshausen
Germany

Mr and Mrs S. Morrison
48, Cambridge Rd
Luton,
Bedfordshire LU 438980939
England

Dear Jane and Steve,

I just wanted to thank you for all the informative articles you sent me about the BBC. I received them yesterday. As you know, I'm giving a talk on the BBC in English and I want to get a good mark.

I really appreciate the time and work you put in to get all that interesting information. It has helped me a lot and I'm sure my talk will go very well because of your help.

Say hello to the children for me.

I'll write or send you an email to tell you how my talk went.

Thanks again!

Best wishes

Alex

Aufgabe 9

Dear Becky,

Sorry I haven't written for so long but we were in the middle of the end of year exams at school. English went well but mathematics was very difficult. It's never been my best subject! I haven't had the results yet but I think I have managed to pass all the exams. I'm so happy they are over. I didn't go out at all for two weeks, not even at the weekends.

Last week I didn't go to school because I caught the flu and had to stay in bed. I had a high temperature and felt terrible. I'm feeling better now although I'm still a bit weak. How are you Becky? Give my regards to your family and write to me soon with all your news.

I promise that I'll try and email you more often in the future.

Lots of love

Nicole

Aufgabe 10

a) Hi Robert!

How about going to the cinema on Friday? There are some good films on at the Multiplex. We could watch the latest Harry Potter film or a comedy with Jack Nicholson. There's also a horror film called *The Omen*. Do you like horror films? Anyway, let me know which film you'd prefer and I'll reserve the seats. All the films start at 8 p.m. so let's meet in front of the cinema at 7:45 p.m.

Shall we go for a drink afterwards? We could go to Harry's Café. It would be nice to have a chat about the film.

See you.

Thomas

b) SMS answer: Great idea! I'd prefer the comedy. See you on Friday at 8 in front of the Multiplex.

Aufgabe 11 a)

1	2	3	4	5	6
B	E	F	D	A	C

b) Max, a sixteen-year-old, greatly dislikes his full name. When a friend visits, his mother calls him by it and uses his friend's full name, too. He wishes she would stop doing this. He wants his mother to behave in a normal way calling him and his friends how they like to be called. He finds her attitude embarrassing and gets very angry about it. *65 words*

Aufgabe 12 The text is about use of the Internet by about a lately calculated number of 100 million people. In the first paragraph experts say that the Internet will soon change all spheres of our lives. The second paragraph deals with e-mails as a very fast and cheap means of communicating by Internet. It is the most important invention since Bell made up the first telephone in 1867.

Ihre Meinung ist uns wichtig!

Ihre Anregungen sind uns immer willkommen. Bitte informieren Sie uns mit diesem Schein über Ihre Verbesserungsvorschläge!

Titel-Nr.	Seite	Vorschlag

Lernen · Wissen · Zukunft
STARK

Bitte hier abtrennen

19-V1M

Bitte ausfüllen und im frankierten Umschlag an uns einsenden. Für Fensterkuverts geeignet.

STARK Verlag
Postfach 1852
85318 Freising

Zutreffendes bitte ankreuzen!

Die Absenderin/der Absender ist:

- ☐ Lehrer/in in den Klassenstufen:
- ☐ Fachbetreuer/in
  Fächer:
- ☐ Seminarlehrer/in
  Fächer:
- ☐ Regierungsfachberater/in
  Fächer:
- ☐ Oberstufenbetreuer/in

- ☐ Schulleiter/in
- ☐ Referendar/in, Termin 2. Staatsexamen:
- ☐ Leiter/in Lehrerbibliothek
- ☐ Leiter/in Schülerbibliothek
- ☐ Sekretariat
- ☐ Eltern
- ☐ Schüler/in, Klasse:
- ☐ Sonstiges:

Unterrichtsfächer: (Bei Lehrkräften)

Absender (Bitte in Druckbuchstaben!)

Kennen Sie Ihre Kundennummer?
Bitte hier eintragen.

Name/Vorname

Straße/Nr.

PLZ/Ort/Ortsteil

Telefon privat   Geburtsjahr

E-Mail

Schule/Schulstempel (Bitte immer angeben!)

Bitte hier abtrennen

Sicher durch alle Klassen!

Lernerfolg durch selbstständiges Üben zu Hause! Die von Fachlehrern entwickelten Trainingsbände enthalten alle nötigen Fakten und viele Übungen mit schülergerechten Lösungen.

Mathematik – Training

Mathematik – Übertritt an weiterführende Schulen	Best.-Nr. 90001
Mathematik 5. Klasse	Best.-Nr. 90005
Mathematik 5. Klasse Baden-Württemberg	Best.-Nr. 80005
Klassenarbeiten Mathematik 5. Klasse	Best.-Nr. 900301
Mathematik 6. Klasse	Best.-Nr. 900062
Bruchzahlen und Dezimalbrüche	Best.-Nr. 900061
Klassenarbeiten Mathematik 6. Klasse	Best.-Nr. 900302
Algebra 7. Klasse	Best.-Nr. 900111
Geometrie 7. Klasse	Best.-Nr. 900211
Klassenarbeiten Mathematik 7. Klasse	Best.-Nr. 900311
Mathematik 8. Klasse	Best.-Nr. 900121
Lineare Gleichungssysteme	Best.-Nr. 900122
Klassenarbeiten Mathematik 8. Klasse	Best.-Nr. 900321
Algebra 9. Klasse	Best.-Nr. 900138
Geometrie 9. Klasse	Best.-Nr. 900221
Klassenarbeiten Mathematik 9. Klasse	Best.-Nr. 900331
Algebra 10. Klasse	Best.-Nr. 90014
Geometrie 10. Klasse	Best.-Nr. 90024
Klassenarbeiten Mathematik 10. Klasse	Best.-Nr. 900341
Potenzen und Potenzfunktionen	Best.-Nr. 900141
Wiederholung Algebra	Best.-Nr. 90009
Wiederholung Geometrie	Best.-Nr. 90010
Kompakt-Wissen Algebra	Best.-Nr. 90016
Kompakt-Wissen Geometrie	Best.-Nr. 90026

Mathematik – Zentrale Prüfungen

VERA 8 – Mathematik Version C: Gymnasium	Best.-Nr. 955082
Bayerischer Mathematik-Test (BMT) Gymnasium 8. Klasse Bayern	Best.-Nr. 950081
Bayerischer Mathematik-Test (BMT) Gymnasium 10. Klasse Bayern	Best.-Nr. 950001
Vergleichsarbeiten Mathematik 7. Klasse Gymnasium Baden-Württemberg	Best.-Nr. 850061
Vergleichsarbeiten Mathematik 9. Klasse Gymnasium Baden-Württemberg	Best.-Nr. 850081
Vergleichsarbeiten Mathematik 11. Klasse Gymnasium Baden-Württemberg	Best.-Nr. 850011
Zentrale Prüfung 2010 Mathematik – ZP 10 Nordrhein-Westfalen	Best.-Nr. 550001
Mittlerer Schulabschluss Mathematik Berlin	Best.-Nr. 111500
Zentrale Prüfung Mathematik 10. Klasse Gymnasium Brandenburg	Best.-Nr. 1250001
Besondere Leistungsfeststellung Mathematik 10. Klasse Gymnasium Sachsen	Best.-Nr. 1450001
Besondere Leistungsfeststellung Mathematik 10. Klasse Gymnasium Thüringen	Best.-Nr. 1650001

Physik

Physik – Mittelstufe 1	Best.-Nr. 90301
Physik – Mittelstufe 2	Best.-Nr. 90302

Deutsch – Training

Leseverstehen 5./6. Klasse	Best.-Nr. 90410
Rechtschreibung und Diktat 5./6. Klasse mit CD	Best.-Nr. 90408
Grammatik und Stil 5./6. Klasse	Best.-Nr. 90406
Aufsatz 5./6. Klasse	Best.-Nr. 90401
Leseverstehen 7./8. Klasse	Best.-Nr. 90411
Grammatik und Stil 7./8. Klasse	Best.-Nr. 90407
Aufsatz 7./8. Klasse	Best.-Nr. 90403
Aufsatz 9./10. Klasse	Best.-Nr. 90404
Deutsche Rechtschreibung 5.–10. Klasse	Best.-Nr. 90402
Übertritt in die Oberstufe	Best.-Nr. 90409
Kompakt-Wissen Rechtschreibung	Best.-Nr. 944065
Kompakt-Wissen Deutsch Aufsatz Unter-/Mittelstufe	Best.-Nr. 904401
Lexikon Deutsch Kinder- und Jugendliteratur	Best.-Nr. 93443

Deutsch – Zentrale Prüfungen

VERA 8 – Deutsch Version C: Gymnasium	Best.-Nr. 955482
Jahrgangsstufentest Deutsch 6. Klasse Gymnasium Bayern	Best.-Nr. 954061
Jahrgangsstufentest Deutsch 8. Klasse Gymnasium Bayern	Best.-Nr. 954081
Zentrale Prüfung 2010 Deutsch – ZP 10 Nordrhein-Westfalen	Best.-Nr. 554001
Mittlerer Schulabschluss Deutsch Berlin	Best.-Nr. 111540
Besondere Leistungsfeststellung Deutsch 10. Klasse Gymnasium Sachsen	Best.-Nr. 1454001
Besondere Leistungsfeststellung Deutsch 10. Klasse Gymnasium Thüringen	Best.-Nr. 1654001

(Bitte blättern Sie um)

Spanisch

Spanisch im 1. Lernjahr	Best.-Nr. 905401
Spanisch im 2. Lernjahr	Best.-Nr. 905402

Englisch Grundwissen

Englisch Grundwissen 5. Klasse	Best.-Nr. 90505
Klassenarbeiten Englisch 5. Klasse mit CD	Best.-Nr. 905053
Englisch Grundwissen 6. Klasse	Best.-Nr. 90506
Klassenarbeiten Englisch 6. Klasse mit CD	Best.-Nr. 905063
Englisch Grundwissen 7. Klasse	Best.-Nr. 90507
Klassenarbeiten Englisch 7. Klasse mit CD	Best.-Nr. 905073
Englisch Grundwissen 8. Klasse	Best.-Nr. 90508
Englisch Grundwissen 9. Klasse	Best.-Nr. 90509
Englisch Grundwissen 10. Klasse	Best.-Nr. 90510
Textproduktion 9./10. Klasse	Best.-Nr. 90541
Englisch Grundwissen Übertritt in die Oberstufe	Best.-Nr. 82453

Englisch Kompakt-Wissen

Kompakt-Wissen Kurzgrammatik	Best.-Nr. 90461
Kompakt-Wissen Grundwortschatz	Best.-Nr. 90464

Englisch Leseverstehen

Leseverstehen 5. Klasse	Best.-Nr. 90526
Leseverstehen 6. Klasse	Best.-Nr. 90525
Leseverstehen 8. Klasse	Best.-Nr. 90522
Leseverstehen 10. Klasse	Best.-Nr. 90521

Englisch Hörverstehen

Hörverstehen 5. Klasse mit CD	Best.-Nr. 90512
Hörverstehen 6. Klasse mit CD	Best.-Nr. 90511
Hörverstehen 7. Klasse mit CD	Best.-Nr. 90513
Hörverstehen 9. Klasse mit CD	Best.-Nr. 90515
Hörverstehen 10. Klasse mit CD	Best.-Nr. 80457

Englisch Rechtschreibung

Rechtschreibung und Diktat 5. Klasse mit 3 CDs	Best.-Nr. 90531
Rechtschreibung und Diktat 6. Klasse mit 2 CDs	Best.-Nr. 90532
Englische Rechtschreibung 9./10. Klasse	Best.-Nr. 80453

Englisch Wortschatzübung

Wortschatzübung 5. Klasse mit CD	Best.-Nr. 90518
Wortschatzübung 6. Klasse mit CD	Best.-Nr. 90519
Wortschatzübung Mittelstufe	Best.-Nr. 90520

Englisch Übersetzung

Translation Practice 1 / ab 9. Klasse	Best.-Nr. 80451
Translation Practice 2 / ab 10. Klasse	Best.-Nr. 80452

Englisch Sprachenzertifikat

Sprachenzertifikat Englisch Niveau A 2 mit Audio-CD	Best.-Nr. 105552
Sprachenzertifikat Englisch Niveau B 1 mit Audio-CD	Best.-Nr. 105550

Englisch: Zentrale Prüfungen

VERA 8 – Englisch Version C: Gymnasium	Best.-Nr. 955582
Jahrgangsstufentest Englisch 6. Klasse mit CD Gymnasium Bayern	Best.-Nr. 954661
Zentrale Prüfung 2010 Englisch – ZP 10 Nordrhein-Westfalen	Best.-Nr. 554601
Mittlerer Schulabschluss Berlin Englisch mit CD	Best.-Nr. 111550
Besondere Leistungsfeststellung Englisch 10. Klasse mit CD Gymnasium Sachsen	Best.-Nr. 1454601
Besondere Leistungsfeststellung Englisch 10. Klasse Gymnasium Thüringen	Best.-Nr. 1654601

Französisch

Französisch im 1. Lernjahr	Best.-Nr. 905502
Rechtschreibung und Diktat 1./2. Lernjahr mit 2 CDs	Best.-Nr. 905501
Französisch im 2. Lernjahr	Best.-Nr. 905503
Französisch im 3. Lernjahr	Best.-Nr. 905504
Französisch im 4. Lernjahr	Best.-Nr. 905505
Wortschatzübung Mittelstufe	Best.-Nr. 94510
Kompakt-Wissen Kurzgrammatik	Best.-Nr. 945011
Kompakt-Wissen Grundwortschatz	Best.-Nr. 905001

Latein

Latein I/II im 1. Lernjahr 5./6. Klasse	Best.-Nr. 906051
Latein I/II im 2. Lernjahr 6./7. Klasse	Best.-Nr. 906061
Latein I/II im 3. Lernjahr 7./8. Klasse	Best.-Nr. 906071
Übersetzung im 1. Lektürejahr	Best.-Nr. 906091
Übersetzung im 2. Lektürejahr	Best.-Nr. 906092
Wiederholung Grammatik	Best.-Nr. 94601
Wortkunde	Best.-Nr. 94603
Kompakt-Wissen Kurzgrammatik	Best.-Nr. 906011

Chemie

Chemie – Mittelstufe 1	Best.-Nr. 90731
Chemie – Mittelstufe 2	Best.-Nr. 90732
Besondere Leistungsfeststellung Chemie 10. Klasse Gymnasium Thüringen	Best.-Nr. 1657301

Biologie

Besondere Leistungsfeststellung Biologie 10. Klasse Gymnasium Thüringen	Best.-Nr. 1657001

Geschichte

Kompakt-Wissen Geschichte Unter-/Mittelstufe	Best.-Nr. 907601

Ratgeber „Richtig Lernen"

Tipps und Lernstrategien – Unterstufe	Best.-Nr. 10481
Tipps und Lernstrategien – Mittelstufe	Best.-Nr. 10482

Bestellungen bitte direkt an:
STARK Verlagsgesellschaft mbH & Co. KG · Postfach 1852 · 85318 Freising
Tel. 0180 3 179000* · Fax 0180 3 179001* · www.stark-verlag.de · info@stark-verlag.de
*9 Cent pro Min. aus dem deutschen Festnetz, Mobilfunk bis 42 Cent pro Min.
Aus dem Mobilfunknetz wählen Sie die Festnetznummer: 08167 9573-0